CREDY

VS

GOOFY

Published by

Wordly Wise Publishers
3rd Floor, 44, Regal Building,
Hanuman Road Area,
Connaught Place,
New Delhi, Delhi – 110001

Web: *https://wordlywise.co.in/*

This book is a work of non-fiction. While every effort has been made to ensure accuracy, certain names, ranks, designations, or details may have been modified for clarity or privacy. The author and publisher have relied on personal accounts, records, and publicly available information, and they make no claim to absolute completeness.

First Published in 2026

ISBN: 978-81-991065-2-9

Praise for *Credy vs Goofy*

I loved Rohit's earlier book *Fall, Don't Fail*, and his latest one has impressed me even more. It's full of relatable stories and thoughtful insights on leadership with authenticity shining throughout the book.

—**Hardeep Singh Brar**, President & CEO, *BMW Group India*

Rohit has a gift for turning everyday moments into powerful leadership lessons you wish you'd learned sooner. The beauty of this book is how the stories stay with you – not as theory, but as ready-to-use tools for the real world.

—**Tarun Garg**, Managing Director and CEO, *Hyundai Motor India Limited*

The 36 concepts presented by Rohit in this book are of exceptional value – each one highly relevant, practical, and firmly anchored in real-world applicability.

—**Jyoti Malhotra**, MD *Volvo Cars India*

I have perused many books on Leadership each with their own insights. What is striking about Rohit's book is its authenticity. Throughout the book Rohit gives anecdotes from his own journey and this makes this book very special, real and inspiring.

—**Shashank Srivastava**, Member, Executive Board,
Maruti Suzuki India Ltd

In an era of jargon-heavy leadership books, Rohit has written something refreshingly human. His stories, research insights and beautiful illustrations make this a must-read for every aspiring leader.

—**Monieka Khanna**, CEO of *Mount Olympus Group of Schools*
and *Founder of IGNISIA*

Rohit has mastered the art of telling it as it is. This book's exploration of the 'tough side' of leadership is courageous and deeply needed. True leadership is not all glory, and he captures that nuance perfectly.

—**Suresh Babu**, Field Service Head,
Maruti Suzuki India Ltd

Having worked closely with Rohit, I can say his leadership lessons are hard-earned. He doesn't teach from theory alone but from the trenches. This book will touch hearts and change mindsets.

—**Kumar Priyesh**, Business Head and Director,
Stellantis India

One of the things I truly appreciated about this book is the thoughtful summary at the end of each chapter. It helps reinforce the key insights so beautifully. And the self-evaluation questions are brilliant – they push you to reflect deeply and apply what you've just read. This makes the book not just informative, but truly transformational.

—**Dhiraj Tripathi**, Chief Business Officer,
Rosmerta Technologies Limited

I absolutely love the concept of 'Credy' in this book. A Credy is someone who radiates true credibility. Rohit brings this idea alive with such simplicity and power that it makes me feel I was always surrounded by such leaders.

—**Ashish Dalia**, CEO, *I Knowledge Factory*

I still remember reading *Fall, Don't Fail* and feeling moved by Rohit's honesty and courage. That book showed us the man behind the leader – vulnerable, reflective and real. This new book feels like the natural next chapter of his journey. It's Rohit, the leader, sharing everything he has lived, learned and practised.

—**Mohit Gupta**, Co-Founder, *FROB*
Friends of Books

Rohit's ability to shine light and identify shadow in leadership makes this book a must read from practical applicability perspective. His humility, rigour, and deep reflections make it an excellent addition to the shelf for anyone entrusted with leading others.

—**Peeyoosh Pandey**, CEO, *Hoonartek*

Rohit has always led with integrity and courage. This book distils decades of those values into actionable insights. I especially loved his stories – real, raw, and relevant to today's leaders.

—**Deepak Mutreja**, Head – Operations,
Suzuki Motorcycles

The Playbook at the end of this book is an absolute gift. It transforms Rohit's insights into a practical self-improvement tool that any leader can start using immediately – it is the perfect way to carry forward the book's wisdom into daily action.

Garima Mittal, Professor, *IIM-Lucknow*

Rohit's writing always strikes me with its raw honesty. In this book, he dissects leadership not as a concept but as a lived experience. The way he has brought out the bright and dark shades is sheer brilliance. Every chapter made me pause and reflect on my own leadership choices.

—**Sachin Samar**, Vice President Environment,
Grasim Industries

The illustrations are beautiful, but it is Rohit's words that lingered with me long after I finished the book. His emphasis on authenticity as the foundation of leadership is precisely what the world needs today.

—**Sheel Sagar**, Head of Sales,
Volkswagen India

The simplicity of language, the authenticity of insights, and the credibility Rohit carries as a leader himself, these make this book unputdownable. His illustrations are delightful and anchor his ideas beautifully.

—**Ankur Seth**, *S*enior Finance Professional

Rohit brings in practical tips to overcome leadership challenges on the strength of his experience & research. The narrative is very engaging & inspires as one moves from one chapter to the next.

—**Rakesh Srivastava**, Former Managing Director of
Nissan India

When Rohit wrote *Fall, Don't Fail*, he inspired many to embrace vulnerability as strength. In this new book, he deepens that exploration further and brings alive the power of authenticity where the leaders chose truth over convenience. He reminds us that courage in leadership isn't just about taking bold decisions but standing tall in truth. His words would inspire many a reader to lead with humility and truth.

—**Sudhir Malhotra**, Former VP – Sales and Marketing,
Renault India

Reading this felt like sitting across a table with a leader who has seen it all – the wins, the failures, and the tough calls no one talks about.

—**Sandeep Tickoo**, Head – Allied Business, *Tata Africa*

This book stands out for its simplicity. The self-evaluation questions at the end of each chapter are particularly useful. They make the reading experience less about theory and more about personal reflection.

—**Deepika Jindal**, General Manager – Strategy, *Timex Group India Limited*

The book's witty illustrations turn each leadership lesson into a visual delight you'll remember long after you put it down.

—**Dr Ankur Kumar Rastogi**, *Avantika University, Ujjain*

The book shines with corporate satire – memorable stories about awkward team-building exercises and presentation fiascos that will have any leader smiling and nodding along.

—**Devopriya Paul**, Global CFO, *Hitachi Energy Transformers*

From the anecdotes to the illustrations, every element of this book pulses with Rohit's passion for genuine leadership. It's a roadmap for anyone eager to lead with authenticity.

—**Satinder Singh Bajwa**, Automobile Industry Veteran

This book brilliantly blends the world of Crediverse with the humorous insights of Goofyland, making leadership lessons both profound and fun.

—**Dr Sarang Kayande**, Mountaineer by passion, Sales and Marketing Professional

Rohit's writing commands attention, and his insights demand action. His book is a generous gift to fellow authors and leaders alike, offering inspiration and practical guidance with every page.

—**Chandni Mathur**, Founder and CEO, *Wordly Wise Publishers*

After *Fall, Don't Fail*, Rohit Goel once again delivers a masterpiece – bold and unfiltered. This book exemplifies the essence of true leadership.

—**Nitin Jain**, CBPO, *Freecharge*

That's Rohit — evolving, inspiring, and always authentic. This book beautifully translates his leadership style into words.

—**Salil Narang**, National Head Customer Relations, *Stellantis*

In a world obsessed with image, Rohit Goel brings leadership back to what truly matters — authenticity, credibility and character.

—**Anand Maithani**, Group Head Global SCM & Manufacturing Planning, *Apollo Tyres Ltd*

Rohit follows *Fall, Don't Fail* with another standout — a book that reminds leaders that credibility is earned daily, through consistency and compassion.

—**Anita Malhotra**, Director Principal, *Lotus Valley International School*

Rohit Goel turns leadership into a daily discipline rather than a distant ideal. Simple, sincere, and beautifully illustrated.

—**Hena Kausar**, Senior Automotive Professional

Few writers capture the soul of leadership as Rohit does. After teaching us how to rise, he now teaches us how to lead with credibility that inspires trust.

—**Gaurav Sharma**, Zonal Head, *Morris Garages India*

Rohit's voice is that of a mentor who's walked the talk and shares it with grace.

—**Sunny Bhat**, Director Sales and Marketing, *GWM Middle East*

Rohit Goel captures what every leader learns the hard way: consistency beats charisma.

—**Anuj Lakhanpal**, Vice President, *Kuehne + Nagel*

Rohit has this rare quality; he leads without ego and mentors without judgement. This book captures that same authenticity we've all experienced working with him.

—**Rahul Agrawal**, Senior Automotive Professional

What I admire most is how Rohit makes excellence feel achievable. He shows that being exceptional isn't about perfection — it's about right intent.

—**Khushboo Singh**, Cluster Principal, *Angel Group of Schools*

Most leadership books tend to romanticise success, painting a picture that feels a little too polished. Rohit's work stands out because it doesn't shy away from the full spectrum of leadership – the triumphs and the struggles, the clarity and the messiness. He approaches both the bright and difficult sides with honesty and empathy, making the lessons feel deeply human. What makes the book powerful is that it blends practical insights you can apply tomorrow with a thoughtful, almost philosophical depth that stays with you.

—**Ankit Dalmia**, Partner, *BCG*

Rohit has a rare talent of turning insightful leadership ideas into conversations that feel natural and engaging rather than academic. This also helps him to turn complex challenges into clear, approachable solutions, making people feel guided, not managed!!!

—**Manish Rathore**, Vice President,
Bajaj Auto

Having worked closely with Rohit, I've seen his authentic leadership shaped by rich corporate experience and many ups and downs. This book is a treasure – honest, inspiring, and packed with practical lessons for real-world leaders.

—**Rajesh Singh**, Founder, *eChargeBays*

Authored by Rohit, whose passion for empowering others shines through every page, this work exemplifies his commitment to making leadership practical and inspiring for all readers. A rare blend of insightful research, compelling storytelling, and actionable advice.

—**Arvind Saxena**, Former President & MD, *General Motors India*,
Former MD, *Volkswagen India*

Managing teams across multiple geographies has taught me one timeless truth – authenticity inspires far more than authority ever can, and this book is a true masterclass in leadership where credibility and compassion go hand in hand.

—**Garima Mittal Misra**, Managing Director,
Group Landmark India

Contents

Exemplary

Protector

Inspirer

Enabler

To all my Credy leaders, for showing me what to do,

and to all my Goofy leaders, for showing me what not to do.

Credibility (kredɪbɪlɪti):

If someone or something has credibility, people believe in them and trust them.

—*Collins Dictionary*

Credibility (kredəˈbɪləti):

The quality that somebody or something has that makes people believe or trust them.

—*Oxford Advanced Learner's Dictionary*

If you don’t believe in the messenger, you won’t believe the message.

—*Kouzes and Posner’s First Law of Leadership*

मेरे नेता कैसे होंगे
अलंकारों से परे
अहंकारों से दूर
पदलोलूप नहीं
पुरस्कार अपेक्षित भी नहीं
ना मान्यताओं की लालसा लिए
ना बहुमत की आस लिए

मेरे नेता कैसे होंगे
गठजोड़ में विफल
चाटुकारिता में असफल
ना उनकी आवाज़ में गर्जना होगी
ना उनके शब्दों में जादू होगा
ना वो सर्वप्रिय होंगे
ना वो सर्वमान्य होंगे
ना होगा उनका ऊँचा सिंहासन
ना होगा उनका महिमा वर्णन

मेरे नेता कैसे होंगे
निश्चय में अकेले
लक्ष्य पे अडिग
लोकनींदा से अभेद्य
जगहँसाई से अविचल
मौलिक विचार लिये
स्वयं के मानक पर खरे

मेरे नेता कैसे होंगे
विश्वसनीय होंगे शब्द उनके
अविश्वसनीय होगी परिस्थिति
आकलन क्षमता उनकी
वे बदलेंगे नहीं किंतु बदल देंगे
स्वयं से परे, तृष्णा से प्रथक

मेरे नेता कैसे होंगे
खराई छलकाते
शुचिता महकाते
आडंबर-रहित
ऊर्जा बिखेरते
मेरे नेता ऐसे होंगे

–रोहित

How should my leaders be?
beyond embellishments
away from egos
expecting no position
seeking no rewards
nor craving approval
or hoping for majority

How should my leaders be?
failed in alliances
inept at sycophancy
there will be no thunder in their voice
nor magic in their words
they will not be everyone's favorite
nor will they be universally accepted
their throne will not be high
there will be no mention of their glories

How should my leaders be?
alone in determination
committed to the goal
impervious to public criticism
unyielding to public mockery
bringing original ideas
living up to their own standards

How should my leaders be?
their words will be reliable
their ability to assess
situations incredible
they will not change but they will change
beyond the self, free from cravings

How should my leaders be?
overflowing with honesty
spreading the fragrance of purity
free of ostentation
radiating energy
This is how my leaders would be.

–Rohit

Author's Introduction

by
Bhuvan Dheer
Executive Officer – Maruti Suzuki India Limited

A Friend, Professional, and Leader: My Two Decades with Rohit

I'VE KNOWN ROHIT for over twenty years now – since 2005. We started as equals, working elbow-to-elbow for a couple of years, forming a deep-seated bond of mutual respect and absolute trust. While I eventually moved to a different location, fate had a funny way of bringing us back together after a major organisational shuffle. I was lucky enough to lead him, and right away, I saw I wasn't just leading a professional, but a future leader.

In the years we worked together, I was constantly struck by Rohit's relentlessly positive attitude and his uncanny knack for bringing truly innovative ideas to the table. Especially when the team was up against a wall, Rohit was the one who consistently delivered exemplary solutions and fresh perspectives that didn't just set benchmarks for us, they became recognised best practices across the industry.

Rohit's dedication never wavered, even during the most gruelling times. Whether it was the long-haul travel to dealerships, representing our company at major conferences, or pushing hard to meet a challenging target, his commitment was always all-in. I vividly recall those late nights: crunching monthly and quarterly plans, finalising month-end reports, and hammering out our next moves. Rohit never asked anyone to do what he wouldn't; he led by example, showing unmatched grit and focus.

What consistently impressed me most, though, was his unwavering support for his team. Rohit never allowed his people to bear the brunt of a challenge alone; he took ownership and ran interference for them, earning the kind of loyalty and respect I have seen few leaders achieve.

Our working relationship was always honest and open. We had countless candid conversations, sometimes agreeing to disagree, but always grounded in mutual respect. Rohit isn't a person who will sugarcoat a tough truth just to save face – he speaks his mind for what's right. That honesty is exactly why our friendship has remained strong even though we haven't worked side-by-side for more than a decade.

Watching Rohit grow as a leader has been pure joy. The people he's mentored have soared to top positions, and he's continuously evolved as a writer, business strategist, and mentor. Despite all his success, he's known for his humility and empathy. His steady, reassuring presence makes everyone around him feel truly seen and valued.

Rohit is a rare leader whose success has only deepened his kindness and approachability. I'm incredibly proud to have worked alongside him, and I wish him nothing but the best in all his future endeavours.

Bhuvan

Foreword

by
Nikhil Sharma
Managing Director – Perfetti Van Melle

IN THE CORPORATE world, few topics have evinced as much interest as Leadership has in recent times. There is plenty of literature, coaching, and training on the subject, and very often contrarian views on what it takes and what it means to be a good leader.

This fascination with leadership is perhaps explained in the two sides it impacts greatly: organisations and employees. Let's look at organisations first. There is enough evidence to suggest that a high proportion of success or wins in companies can be directly attributed to great leadership. By corollary, if results are not good, the leader must be held accountable, and this is why talent at top level is sought after.

Now let's look at employees. Almost everyone who joins the workforce wants a team to lead as they move up the corporate ladder. There is an ambition to rise professionally, a desire to earn more, and perhaps a need for validation of ability.

If we think about it, the two principal players who have a keen interest in leadership are chasing outcomes that don't necessarily overlap. There are times, however, when this happens – when the organisation and the individual are both devoted to the same cause – and those are the stories that get told and repeated.

I am therefore delighted (and very pleasantly surprised and quite intimidated) that Rohit has asked me to write an introduction to his labour of love. It's a subject he is passionate about and, in my experience, magic is always created when passion meets hard work and strong rigour. Rohit and I are batchmates from Engineering (a long time ago in a galaxy far, far away). I have been following his success as a writer and I'm immensely proud of what he has achieved.

The book centres on the woefully ignored and rarely practised concept of Credibility in leadership. To drive home the point, Rohit has distilled the larger concept into 36 Mantras drawn from his own experiences as a leader. Reading each chapter feels like wisdom is converted into grounded lessons. The characters of Credy and Goofy, representing credible and not-so-credible leaders Rohit has met in his life, add a touch of humour and make the content relatable and interesting.

At the end of the book there is a Credification Playbook to help you evaluate and rank your own leadership style and become a more credible leader.

Before I hand you over to Rohit, I am tempted to share some ideas from the book that resonated with me. Stuff that I try and do (very often not very well) and that has contributed to my success.

- **Honouring Commitments:** There are leaders who quietly inspire others by the simple and underrated act of honouring their word. They stay true to their commitments regardless of circumstances. These are the leaders that particularly stand out to me and that I have grown to admire over the course of my career.
- **Easy Exits:** Today more than ever, emotional intelligence is seen as a quintessential trait of good leadership. One of the most remarkable reflections of this is how a leader handles the exit process when a subordinate decides to leave.

In my own experience, when I want to know the person behind the leader, I observe how they behave with team members serving a notice period.

- **Futile Meetings, Empty Results, and the Illusion of Work:** There is a certain kind of power attached to calling meetings, and some leaders thrive on the ego trip. The truth is, if we removed a third of all meetings a leader attends in a month, work would still get done, and people may even get more productive. I like to run a tight ship with clear agendas and rigorous follow-ups, and I'm glad Rohit has dedicated an entire chapter to this.

I have had the fortune in my career to learn from the best and I stand now on the shoulders of giants who came before me. When I reported to them, there were times when I would think to myself, 'When I come to their position, I would do this differently.' Now, I often think, 'If they were here, what would they do?' The dichotomy of these statements is perhaps my strongest argument to you for reading this book. I hope you enjoy it as much as I have!

Congratulations and really well done Rohit! Keep shining.

Nikhil Sharma

Introduction

AT AN EVENT around my debut book, *Fall, Don't Fail*, a young woman in the audience asked me a question that stopped me in my thoughts: 'What makes a leader a great one?'

When I asked her to elaborate, she added, 'How are some leaders able to generate unwavering devotion in their teams? What is that X-factor that some leaders have and others don't?'

While I did answer her questions with whatever came to my mind in that moment, they continued to linger in my head for days afterwards. When did I first feel that kind of devotion for a leader? And just as important, when did I feel the opposite – disenchantment with my leader's conduct? In other words, what truly sets great leaders apart?

I was reminded of a recent conversation with some friends and former colleagues. Satyam had shared a story of a leader who never took responsibility, blaming everyone else when targets weren't met. Rahul had mentioned how his boss owned every mistake and setback, earning the respect of her team. Shivani had recounted her own experience with an undisciplined and insecure leader who excelled at creating a toxic culture.

My own life and career have given me a front-row seat to both wonderful and disastrous leadership styles. As I pored over those experiences, the answer soon became clear. It isn't great technical skills or even visionary brilliance that make a great leader. The key difference lies in something else: how leaders establish themselves as authentic and trustworthy.

This realisation took me back to two things: people and incidents.

The People

I recalled many leaders, some of whom I had known personally and others that I admired as national figures. There were a few who stood out, and I placed them in two groups:

Group 1

- A national sports captain who led a team of underdogs to a World Cup victory. On receiving the trophy, he immediately handed it over to his teammates. And when it was time for the group photograph, he stood quietly at a corner, giving his team a chance to bask in the limelight.
- A national political leader who faced unending adversity yet never compromised his principles. While he mentored countless leaders and helped them grow in both wisdom and stature, he never himself took a position of prominence. Nor did he ever chase privilege or recognition for his sacrifices. He died a martyr.
- A chief of sales and marketing with a humble educational background and modest beginnings, who was now leading thousands. She was deeply admired for upholding her own standards of honesty and integrity that went far beyond the organisation's rule book. Every now and then, she would send an email to her team sharing the do's and don'ts she applied to her own conduct.

Group 2

- The founder of a unicorn start-up making billions of dollars and growing year on year. The company had a workforce of over ten thousand people, but this leader was despised by much of his workforce. Why? Because he was never trustworthy when it came to his people's future. Under his leadership, random transfers, mass dismissals, and unceremonious exits were as common as day and night.
- The CEO of an NGO, supposedly uplifting the underprivileged through education, with dozens of teachers devoted to the cause. The organisation was being funded by blue-chip companies and philanthropists. On the surface, everything looked admirable. Yet, behind closed doors, the leader referred to his own teachers as 'a herd of sheep that needs to be canned every now and then to keep them on track'.
- An accomplished sportsperson who had become a professional coach after retirement. But instead of building a strong team, he loved playing the politics of divide and rule. With his petty politics, he created rifts in the very team he was hired to train.

Did you notice the similarities and differences among these two sets of leaders? The similarity is that all of them were successful individuals holding positions of influence. The difference is in how they led and the impact their respective leadership styles had on their followers.

In my professional journey, I have met both kinds of leaders and many who fall somewhere in between. Whenever I reflect on my experiences, I feel a tremendous sense of gratitude towards those leaders. Exceptional, mediocre, or downright terrible – every leader taught me something: qualities and behaviours I should embrace, and others that are best avoided. These lessons have shaped me not just as a leader but as a human being.

The Incidents: A Leader's Persona and Its Impact on People

A leader's persona directly impacts the fate, fame, and fortunes of those he leads. This persona is not built overnight, but created bit by bit through the leader's decisions, actions, and reactions, all of which bring out his true character and characteristics.

I can recall many instances where a leader's persona profoundly influenced his team's ability to perform, but one experience stands out dramatically.

I once reported to two very different leaders in the same organisation. In hindsight, I had completely contrasting mindsets and ways of operating during those two periods, much like white and black. So let's call them the 'white period' and the 'black period'.

During the white period, I was super committed to my work and went out of my comfort zone to achieve my targets, sometimes even exceeding them by a big margin.

There was also excellent bonhomie within the team, with everyone lending a hand to help others meet their goals. We gladly took on extra responsibilities and did not mind spending a few extra hours in the office when needed. All in all, we were proud of our work and devoted to the organisation. There was no insecurity, no desperation to hog the limelight. And this was all because we had a leader who was not only a great visionary but also authentic, hard-working, and trustworthy.

I fondly remember how I would wear my uniform with great pride and flaunt it in society. If anyone in my social circle criticised our brand based on a personal experience, I would defend it staunchly, explaining the overall value proposition while acknowledging that individual experiences may differ. In every sense, I was devoted to my work and so were most of my colleagues.

This idyllic state lasted a few years, but then came the disruption. A new leader took over the team and everything changed. The white period ended and the black period started. Within just a few months, we completely disintegrated as a team.

This new leader wasn't particularly bad at strategising, but his approach to leading people was seriously flawed and laced with distrust. Making us feel insecure, instigating us to pick fights with each other, hiring and promoting mediocre talent, withholding important information – these were just a few of his toxic traits.

Before long, the entire team was on edge because of this leader. The once vibrant atmosphere was now a pale shadow of the past. Genuine smiles turned into fake ones. The feeling of being a team, a unit, was simply gone.

A sense of insecurity had crept in, and people started avoiding any work they could. The focus shifted to chasing tasks and goals that gave high visibility. Team conversations changed from discussing milestones to discussing bonuses and increments. For many, money became the only motivation to stay. People joked with each other, 'Don't take so much trouble. Just take your pay cheque and be happy.'

A lot of 'corner of the office' talks started taking place. While people still admired the organisation in public, private conversations were full of cynicism and frustration. The sense of belonging we once felt for the company was gone. Inevitably, this black period saw an exodus of talent.

The one and only reason behind all of this: passing of the baton to our new leader. While his predecessor enjoyed an almost legendary status among us, this leader had miserably failed to earn our trust.

In essence, there had been a big shift in how we perceived our leader, and that influenced all our thoughts and actions.

Across my twenty-seven-year career, I have had many such contrasting experiences, and they have influenced my own evolution as a leader. Looking back, the leaders I admired, worked for like a devotee, or followed almost like a cult shared one common trait: they were all enormously credible leaders – extraordinary beings who consciously built their *credibility*. It was pious to them, spiritual even, and completely non-negotiable.

If I were to summarise all of this learning into a few words, it would be this: no matter how good a leader is at strategy, execution, hard work, or anything else, the one quality that truly separates great leaders from the rest is credibility.

Before I get into the what and how of credible leadership, let me first talk about what we mean by 'credibility' and 'leadership'.

As defined at the beginning of this book, credibility is the quality that makes a leader believable and trustworthy. In turn, everything the leader thinks, says, and does builds or breaks his credibility.

And what do we mean by leadership? Giving orders? No. Getting your work done? No, again. Having a long list of loyalists? Not really. So then, what is leadership?

Leadership, as I see it, is an individual's ability to ignite in others a genuine desire to perform. This desire is not forced by the leader's position, authority, or age; it comes from within. When authentic, this desire translates into the right attitude, inspiring people to do the right thing even when no one is watching, even when all they are doing is following the leader's gut feeling, and even when there is no reward for doing the right thing – and no penalty for not doing it.

To me, that is real leadership.

Beyond my own experiences, I continue to spot credible leaders in many other fields – sports, politics, business, arts and literature, the military, technology, and others. These leaders are a rarity not because of their talent or achievements, but because of that rarest of rare quality: credibility!

My Formula for Great Leadership

My exploration of the art and science of great leadership led me to reflect on my own leadership style. Along the way, I read extensively on the topic, spoke with other leaders, and even ran opinion polls to get a wider perspective.

Remarkably, almost everyone I interviewed agreed that credibility is key to a solid leader-follower relationship. And yet, very few had actively thought about building their credibility as leaders.

I also found that most literature on the subject still focuses on conventional wisdom – strategy, vision, organising ability, execution skills, communication skills, experience, and so on. These skills are invaluable, no doubt, but there's rarely any mention of credibility.

No school, college, or leadership programme talks about this all-important aspect of leadership. In fact, most leadership courses are marred by dated curriculum and theoretical frameworks that don't always apply to real-world scenarios.

With the conviction that credibility is one of the defining qualities of a successful leader, I set out to try and understand how one can become a credible leader. While I have baked all my research into the chapters ahead, let me share a simple yet powerful formula I arrived at in the process.

$$\textbf{Leadership} = \begin{bmatrix} \textbf{Vision + Strategy + Hard work} \\ \textbf{+ Execution + Competence} \end{bmatrix} \times \textbf{Credibility}$$

Here's what it means: while a visionary outlook, strategic thinking, hard work, executional abilities, and technical competence are all important to be a successful leader, it is credibility that makes good leaders great. Credibility is the powerful multiplier that can swing a leader's effectiveness in either direction – high or low.

At this point, I would like you to pause and reflect on the leaders in your own life – your parents, teachers, coaches, and bosses. Think about what you wanted from these individuals and how they influenced you and why. Then, ask yourself, 'Who among them would I want to lead or mentor my own children or loved ones?' Your answer will reveal credibility as the paramount quality you seek in a leader.

Credibility is the ultimate goal you should chase to be the leader you aspire to become. A leader who is honest in his word and actions. A leader who does what he says. A leader who is authentic, protective, and inspiring. A leader who holds himself to the highest personal standards.

I have written this book with the spirit and conviction that we can create many more credible leaders by helping people make tiny – and some not so tiny – changes in the way they lead.

Credy and Goofy: An Introduction

The credible and not-so-credible leaders I have met in my life appear in this book by the names Credy and Goofy.

Credys: These are leaders with sky-high credibility and a near-perfect credibility score. They are confident yet humble, objective yet sensitive, demanding yet protective. But most of all, they are trustworthy and well-intentioned. Every action and decision of these leaders is accepted with great joy and will by their followers. Successes and failures are very much a part of their work, but their credibility outshines any results whatsoever.

Goofys: You're right in thinking that the name comes from 'goofing up'! Sometimes these leaders goof up deliberately, driven by ill intentions, and sometimes out of sheer stupidity or lack of foresight. Mind you, they are not always bad people, just bad leaders who fail to rise above the basic human tendencies of insecurity, ego, lethargy, and confused vision.

The words, actions, and decisions of these leaders are rarely in sync. They reach leadership positions not by merit, but by virtue of passage of time or lack of a better alternative. As a result, many are leaders only by title or designation.

Forget about devotion, these leaders command little respect from their subordinates. Working under them feels more like a duty, utterly devoid of any joy, excitement, or inspiration.

Let's now proceed to some related terms you will encounter in the book:

- *Credi(uni)verse*: the universe of people, processes, and culture created by a Credy leader
- *Goofiland*: an unhealthy space of people, processes, and culture created by a Goofy leader

- *Credism*: the quality of being a Credy leader
- *Goofism*: the state of being a Goofy leader
- *Crediniyat*: the intent and motives of a Credy leader
- *Goofaniyat*: the intent and motives of a Goofy leader
- *Credified*: the positive transformation of people shaped by a Credy leader
- *Goofified*: the negative impact on people caused by a Goofy leader.

How This Book Is Structured

This book is a compilation of 36 Credibility Mantras divided into four categories: Exemplary, Protector, Inspirer, and Enabler.

Each chapter starts with a brief introduction to set the context, followed by a deep dive into why and how to implement the mantra. The discussion is punctuated with anecdotes and illustrations, and each chapter concludes with key takeaways. Finally, a self-evaluation section invites you to honestly assess yourself or others on a credibility scale.

The Credification Playbook

The Credification Playbook provided at the end of the book will be your companion in this journey. It includes:

- *Diagnosis and Adoption Tool*: This tool will help you assess your leadership style, calculate your Credible Leadership Behaviour (CLB) score, and create an action plan to enhance your credibility as a leader.
- *Credimeter*: Divided into three zones – Credy Zone, Croofy Zone, and Goofy Zone – this tool will help you interpret your CLB score and get deeper insight into your leadership behaviour.

How This Book Will Benefit You

- You will discover how to become an incredible leader by being credible.
- You will learn the 36 essential traits of a Credy leader.
- Through anecdotes in each chapter, you will get to know how real-life leaders operate.
- The Credification Playbook will help you track your transformation into a Credy leader.

Before you take your first step on this journey of learning and discovery, pause for a moment. Close your eyes and think of the word *leader*. Who comes to mind? Is it your boss at work, a prominent political figure, a sports captain, the head of a group you belong to? Now, think about the words you would use to describe this leader.

Some examples: visionary, bold, timid, honest, dishonest, good, bad, stupid, genius, trustworthy, crooked, collaborative, quarrelsome, motivating, demotivating, respectful, spineless, exceptional, partial.

With this introspective exercise, you may have visualised a carousel of people you see as leaders. Think about why you associated certain words with a particular individual.

Now, reverse the gaze. Think about your own team and honestly consider what they think of you as their leader. Is there a big gap in how they perceive you and how you would like to be perceived? This book promises to be your guide to bridging that gap.

While writing this book, I have made every effort to be pragmatic. Everything you will read in these pages is based on my decades of experience working with leaders, whom I observed with great interest. I have also been in leadership roles myself and have put those lessons into practice.

While the ideas presented here are simple to understand, implementing them won't be as easy, unless you're truly committed to becoming a credible leader. Getting a leadership position can sometimes be a matter of chance, but being a successful, respected leader is a matter of cultivated magic – the magic of inspiring unwavering loyalty and trust among your followers.

This book is a call to action for anyone who has struggled with leadership – whether as a follower who has suffered at the hands of poor leadership or as a leader who wants to become a better leader.

References to Indian Cinema

In India, the cinema is an integral part of our lives and culture, and I'm a big fan myself. To add a touch of fun, I've included iconic dialogues from Hindi films that complement the content of the chapters.

I realise that some readers may not be familiar with these films or dialogues, but I hope you will enjoy them and even be intrigued to look them up. If nothing, they might become a conversation starter with your family or colleagues.

A Note on the Leaders Referenced in This Book

For confidentiality, I have chosen not to name the real-life leaders referenced in this book. While I would like to celebrate and acknowledge the Credys I have encountered, I do not wish to name and shame the Goofys. However, this will not affect your reading experience in any way.

A Note on Pronouns

This book uses male pronouns (he, him, his) when referring to leaders. This is purely for narrative consistency and does not reflect any bias or discrimination. Leadership is for everyone, and the leadership qualities discussed here are not exclusive to any particular gender. My goal is to tell a story that inspires readers of all backgrounds.

With the stage set, let's dive into the world of Credy and Goofy, and see what these true accounts can teach us about credible leadership.

Exemplary

'Main aaj bhi pheke hue paise nahin uthata.'

'Parampara, Pratishtha, Anushasan, Yeh is gurukul ke teen stambh hai.'

1/36

Leading with High Personal Standards

In any line of work, leaders get many opportunities to abuse the system for their personal gains. The degree of restraint a leader exercises in these situations, especially when he cannot be questioned, is what sets apart exceptional leaders from the weaklings. While Goofys don't mind trading their credibility for small gains, Credys will go to any extent to protect their personal integrity, even if it means defying the status quo. These leaders will never say yes to easy money or personal favours if it compromises their integrity.

How a leader behaves in sinfully alluring situations not only reveals his own true character but sets the standard for others to follow. Credible leaders uphold high personal standards in three critical areas: discipline, ethics, and integrity.

Each organisation has its own norms, customs, and standards, but the lines around them are not always black and white. As a result, certain practices may not go down well with every leader.

A Credy may find them too relaxed, and a Goofy may see them as too restrictive. So it often becomes a matter of personal choice for the leader.

In my career, I have seen leaders exhibit surprisingly contrasting behaviours when it comes to following a personal value system. I will start with Credys.

Since Credys are in the game for the long run, they are particularly conscious of their personal brand both within and outside the organisation. If the situation so demands, they will not hesitate to deviate from the established code of conduct to set even more stringent rules of their own, as demonstrated by my Credy leader in the following example.

I once worked in an organisation where vendors regularly flattered company officers with gifts. Our leader, who had recently joined us as the regional sales head, also received some gifts around Diwali. On the eve of Diwali break, his assistant took the presents to his car for him to take home. When our leader learned of this, he asked for all the items to be brought back to his office. He then wrote a personal note to each vendor and instructed his assistant to return the gifts.

While our company policy allowed us to accept Diwali gifts worth up to five hundred rupees from vendors, this was not acceptable to our leader. 'Why do we need gifts from vendors at all?' he questioned. Well, we all know why vendors send gifts to company officials!

Later, this Credy sent a polite but assertive email to all our vendors, informing them that our office would no longer accept favours of even one rupee in value.

This solid-gold behaviour by our leader raised the bar for all of us. It brought a cultural shift in the team. Our vendors, too, started treating us with more respect. But there was another, indirect benefit: not accepting undue favours from stakeholders greatly improved our power of negotiation. While earlier we were always under pressure to oblige our vendors, now we were always on higher ground when dealing with them. A simple decision by our new leader had completely changed the game.

Goofys, on the other hand, are a greedy lot who cannot resist the temptation of freebies. One of my leaders was a living example of this. Bizarrely, he kept a list of all the gifts he received during the year and allotted business based on the value of the item received. Not just this, he frequently went out for drinks and dinner with our vendors in the name of building relationships, but everyone knew that his only motive was to have a good time at their expense. Naturally, this gave our vendors the power to dictate terms.

Even the caterer who supplied food to our office acted like he was invincible, for he was one of the biggest freebie suppliers to this Goofy. The quality and service of his food were both pathetic, but he got away with it because he organised lavish personal parties for our leader.

As the saying goes, vices, like virtues, come in bunches. Not only did our Goofy leader have zero integrity, he was also highly undisciplined. His business trips were more like luxury vacations, with a few meetings thrown in to impress his bosses. On these trips, he would start working only at noon, after a lavish breakfast, and wind up by four.

You can well imagine our reaction when this Goofy tried to lecture us on the value of hard work. None of us took him seriously. Who wants to follow a leader who talks north and walks south?

Goofys don't seem to realise that their misconduct earns them the lifetime title of a weak character with low morals. If Credys believe in the idiom 'Practise before you preach', a Goofy's version would be 'Preach, then breach!' Maybe this explains why Credys have admirers even in their absence, while Goofys have a room full of haters wherever they go.

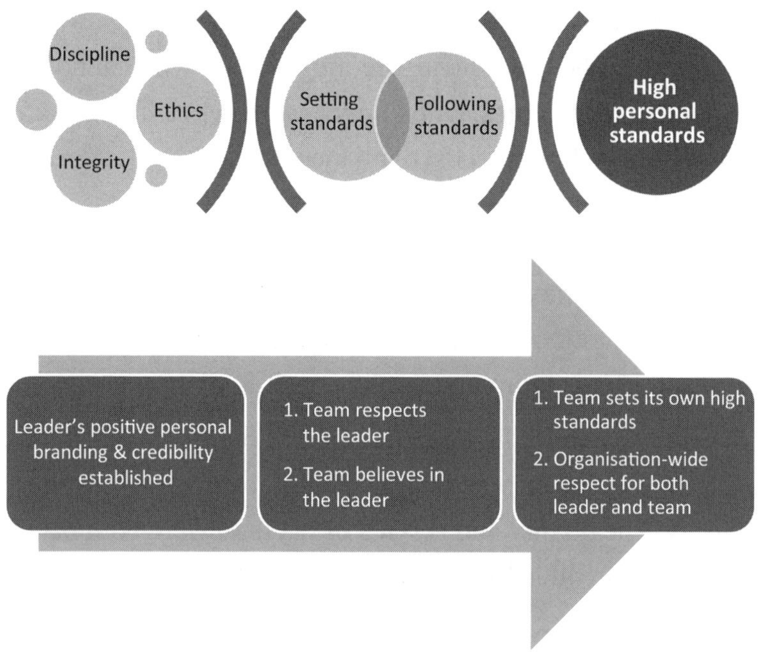

FIGURE 1: **Cause and Effect of High Personal Standards**

Key Takeaways

- If you want to rise as a leader, kill your greed, because the hidden cost of fulfilling your greed through corrupt methods is backbreakingly high.
- If you see an unethical practice, call it out. If there are loopholes in your organisation's ethical standards, fix them. If required, set new rules that supersede conventional practices.
- Rise above mediocrity, and never trade your integrity for material gains.

- Cement your credibility by making ethical decisions. Show the world that you don't have a price tag plastered to your forehead.

Self-Evaluation

Reflect on your personal standards around discipline, ethics, and integrity. Evaluate yourself with the following questions:

- Are you aware that your personal value system directly affects your credibility as a leader?
- Do you believe that leaders must display high personal standards before they can demand the same from their team members?
- Do you realise that your conduct has a direct and definitive impact on the conduct of team members?
- Would you go against an accepted practice if it doesn't agree with your personal value system?

Now, give yourself Credy Points based on your behaviour in the above context. Pick the appropriate option:

- ○ Always behave like a Credy: 10 Credy points
- ○ Mostly behave like a Credy: 7 Credy points
- ○ Sometimes behave like a Credy, sometimes like a Goofy: 4 Credy points
- ○ Always behave like a Goofy: 0 Credy points

*'Ek baar jo maine commitment kar di,
to fir main apne aap ki bhi nahi sunta.'*

2/36

Honouring Commitments: A Matter of Life and Death

ALL LEADERS ARE expected to work towards certain goals, often without any guarantee of a successful outcome. Despite this uncertainty, credible leaders do everything in their power to meet their goals. In this situation, where people simply trust their leader and follow him without question, the leader must do everything in his capacity to honour his commitments. In other words, a leader can command respect and generate response only if he's seen as someone who 'walks the talk'.

While popular culture will have us believe otherwise, in real life people don't look for big talks or lofty promises from their leaders. What they really want is a leader who translates his words into action. The most admired leaders consciously work on this trait and, in turn, cultivate a loyal following for life.

Credy leaders treat their commitments as sacrosanct. For them, standing by their word isn't up for negotiation – if they made a promise, be it to a client, a vendor, another department, or their own team members, it must be fulfilled. These leaders know that nothing damages their personal integrity and reputation more than failing to uphold their word. Working within the limitations of their role, they adopt a do-or-die approach to deliver what they promised.

A Credy leader I once had at a renowned car manufacturing company took this ideology to another level. This was a big company that sold its vehicles through a country-wide dealer network. Dealers are business partners who provide manufacturers with the wherewithal (infrastructure, workforce, working capital, etc.) to sell their products to end consumers. There are typically multiple dealers in a city.

To avoid competition among our dealer-partners and maintain harmony, our company had established a set of rules for all dealers to follow. To ensure compliance within his territory, my leader fixed a penalty of five lakh rupees for defaulters. This was done in agreement with our dealer-partners.

As it happened, one dealership repeatedly flouted a rule, but when confronted, they refused to accept their mistake or pay the penalty. Now this was a tricky situation for my leader. A rule set by him was being blatantly disregarded, undermining his authority. With a dealer conference coming up soon, we were concerned that other dealers would bring up the issue and demand action against this dealer.

While we braced ourselves for the worst, our leader came up with a unique solution to the problem. On the day of the event, before the situation could get out of hand, he placed a personal cheque of five lakh rupees on the table. Then he made an announcement, 'If the defaulting dealer doesn't pay the penalty today, I will pay on his behalf. My credibility is at stake here, and it's more important to me than any amount of money.'

The gesture surprised many, but it had the desired effect. Not only did the erring dealer pay up the same day, but the issue of non-compliance never arose again, at least during my tenure with the company.

When we asked our leader how he came up with such an unprecedented move, he said that he had barely slept the previous few nights. As the one responsible for enforcing the rules, his integrity was on the line, and his commitment to the dealer fraternity had to be honoured at any cost. He admitted that taking five lakh rupees out of his personal savings would have been difficult, but no amount of money had any worth when his credibility was in question. Some of us teased him for his rather dramatic style, and we all had a good laugh.

All said and done, his actions that day paid off well. He came to be known as a leader whose word was as good as a guarantee, and we earned the reputation of a team that followed through on its commitments no matter what.

For me, what made this incident memorable was my leader's decision to take personal responsibility when he could have easily blamed the defaulting dealer and moved on. But true Credys rarely take the easy route. They choose what is right over what is convenient, even when the outcome may not be fully in their favour.

On the other hand, Goofys are by and large indifferent to their commitments. I have met two types of Goofys in this regard. First are those who make commitments but then conveniently forget to follow up, thereby failing to deliver their part of the bargain. Then there are those I call 'wilful defaulters', who make commitments with no intention of ever honouring them.

I once worked with a Goofy who was notorious for making commitments that far exceeded his authority or capacity. His modus operandi was to make short-term gains by making unrealistic promises to our dealer-partners, like a higher marketing budget, reduced sales targets, extra incentives, penalty waivers, and so on. Those dealers, in turn, would look to us to fulfil our Goofy leader's commitments.

Trusting this Goofy's words, dealers and vendors organised events or ran promotions for which reimbursements were never paid. When asked for clarification, he would blatantly deny ever having made those commitments. These gimmicks destroyed not only his own credibility but also the team's image as the face of the company. Dealers openly started saying that they did not trust us and insisted on written communication for the smallest of matters.

This Goofy did not even spare his own team. A habitual liar, to use us more and more, he would routinely promise us salary hikes, promotions, choice transfers, and plum postings, only to never follow through on his word.

Interestingly, Goofys think of themselves as a smart lot for manipulating others into fulfilling their demands. But when it's their own turn to deliver, they resort to lies and excuses. But they forget a simple fact – breaking promises ruins their reputation and destroys their credibility among one and all. Such leaders are distrusted not only by their immediate colleagues but also by others they may never have interacted with. As someone rightly said, reputation travels!

Effectiveness of a leader $\propto$ Face value of a leader

Face value of a leader $\propto$ Honouring of commitments by leader

Hence,

Effectiveness of a leader $\propto$ Honouring of commitments by leader

---

FIGURE 2: **The Leadership Believability Equation**

Key Takeaways

- As a leader, it should be your second nature to commit only what you can deliver and then to make it happen. With this approach, you will build allies for life who will trust your words like they're cast in stone.

- Remember, it's all right to commit less. People will not care that you didn't promise them the moon, but they will be merciless if you are callous with your words.
- Honouring commitments – this trait is easily the foundation of Credy behaviour. Of course, it will not always be smooth sailing. Sometimes, circumstances will have changed since you made the commitment, or a genuine difficulty may tempt you away from doing the right thing. In these moments, remind yourself: being branded a liar and a promise-breaker is a stigma that is impossible to shed.

Self-Evaluation

Reflect on how much you value your own word as a leader and whether you know the importance of fulfilling your commitments. Evaluate yourself with the following questions:

- Do you consistently follow through on your commitments to your colleagues, clients, and external partners?
- Do you ensure that your team members do not overcommit and fulfil what they promised?
- Do you track your unfulfilled commitments and the reasons behind them?
- Do you realise that the integrity of your words is paramount to your reputation?

Now, give yourself Credy Points based on your behaviour in the above context. Pick the appropriate option:

- ○ Always behave like a Credy: 10 Credy points
- ○ Mostly behave like a Credy: 7 Credy points
- ○ Sometimes behave like a Credy, sometimes like a Goofy: 4 Credy points
- ○ Always behave like a Goofy: 0 Credy points

'Johny bure kaam toh karta hai lekin imaan ke saath.'

3/36

The Credy-Goofy Divide: Transparency versus Manipulation

FAILURES, SETBACKS, AND non-achievements are a part of any work environment. Regardless of the outcome, every performance comes under scrutiny sooner or later, where you are expected to present the results and their analysis to your stakeholders. When showcasing performance, strong leaders present the facts with utmost honesty, no matter how grim those facts are. In contrast, weakhearted or cunning leaders try to hide the real picture by twisting the facts and highlighting fake achievements. There cannot be a bigger credibility breaker than falsifying the facts, and yet many leaders do it on purpose and without remorse.

In business, as in life, good results usher in good times while poor performance brings bad times for all involved. This is a harsh but practical reality of the workplace. In either scenario, it is the leader who has to present his team's performance at various forums.

Presenting to a large audience that is going to judge you solely on your performance is no easy task, and it's especially difficult when results have been below expectations. It becomes a critical test of the leader's credibility. Leaders who believe that their team worked sincerely are at ease presenting to any group. They fearlessly give an honest account of where the team stands on each deliverable, along with the challenges faced, actions taken, and mistakes made along the way.

But not all leaders have the courage, confidence, or desire to be authentic in these situations. Some resort to low-level tactics that are well known in any industry – fudge the data, show a few isolated wins as a trend, misquote others, and blame failure on other people or random factors.

I have experienced both scenarios in my career. Let me start with the positive one.

With our annual sales conference around the corner, I was working with my leader to prepare a presentation on our team's performance over the previous year. For various reasons, our sales figures had been particularly bad that year. We had missed our annual target by a significant margin. But my leader, a thorough Credy, had no intention of whitewashing the facts. His instructions were clear: there should be no window dressing, no manipulation of data, no false statements – only pure, authentic analysis.

Now, this Credy was no novice. He knew the potential repercussions of sharing our actual figures with the entire organisation. But his logic was clear: one bad year could be recovered, but credibility, once lost, could never be earned back. To get us all on the same page, he called a team meeting and explained his thought process to my colleagues.

On the day of the event, as he took the stage to address a hall packed with colleagues, seniors, and internal stakeholders, we all joined him to show our support. He confidently stated the facts, explaining the numbers and the reasons behind them, and concluded with an action plan to recover from the setback.

Of course, we did not receive an applause for our brilliant analysis of the results, but we could sense the audience's admiration for our leader's transparent and candid presentation. Because of him, we too stood there with honesty and pride, rather than with the shame of fabricating blatant lies. We might have fallen short on the results, but we had protected our all-important *credibility*.

Those five or six days of working closely with my leader was a memorable experience. I felt a profound sense of liberation – one that comes from being honest even when the odds are stacked against you.

Fast-forward to a similar situation a few years later. This time I had a leader who was the poster boy of *Goofism*. To start with, this Goofy simply refused to acknowledge that we had failed on most of our deliverables that quarter. He was obsessed with portraying himself as a winner, and he was willing to go to any lengths for it. On his orders, data was falsified, poor sales were wrongly attributed to logistics, and dirty tricks were played to shift blame to other people or circumstances.

When presenting the results, he tried his usual tactic of diverting attention to less important matters, but the audience was no fool. We could see their frowns and muted displeasure as he spoke. The moment he stopped talking, they started asking questions that made us feel like we were being persecuted in public. It was a day of massive embarrassment for us, with a rival team even calling us 'a bunch of fakes'.

Looking back at these two leaders now, it doesn't surprise me how differently their careers panned out. While my Credy leader went up the ranks to become the youngest-ever executive in his organisation, Goofy ended up a rolling stone, moving from one company to another before he was finally ousted on integrity issues.

There was also a remarkable difference in the followership of these leaders. Working under Credy gave me and my colleagues the confidence to openly acknowledge the realities of our work. A missed target, a dip in performance, a mistake here and there, all was okay as long as we gave our hundred per cent and worked with intention and commitment. It was a great atmosphere to be in, and it earned our leader a solid and loyal following. A quote from the film What Women Want (2000) sums it up: 'No games, just sports'.

In contrast, my Goofy leader had few genuine supporters, and most of them were manipulative Goofys themselves – adept at distorting facts rather than doing trailblazing work.

If you, too, have a tendency to cover up facts like a Goofy, remember that they are like skeletons in the closet that will come back to haunt you sooner or later. And colleagues who helped you bury those skeletons will always know where to find them – a weakness that can be used against you at any time.

But when you are truthful like a Credy, you will have no fear of being exposed. No one will ever be able to say to you, 'I know what you did!'

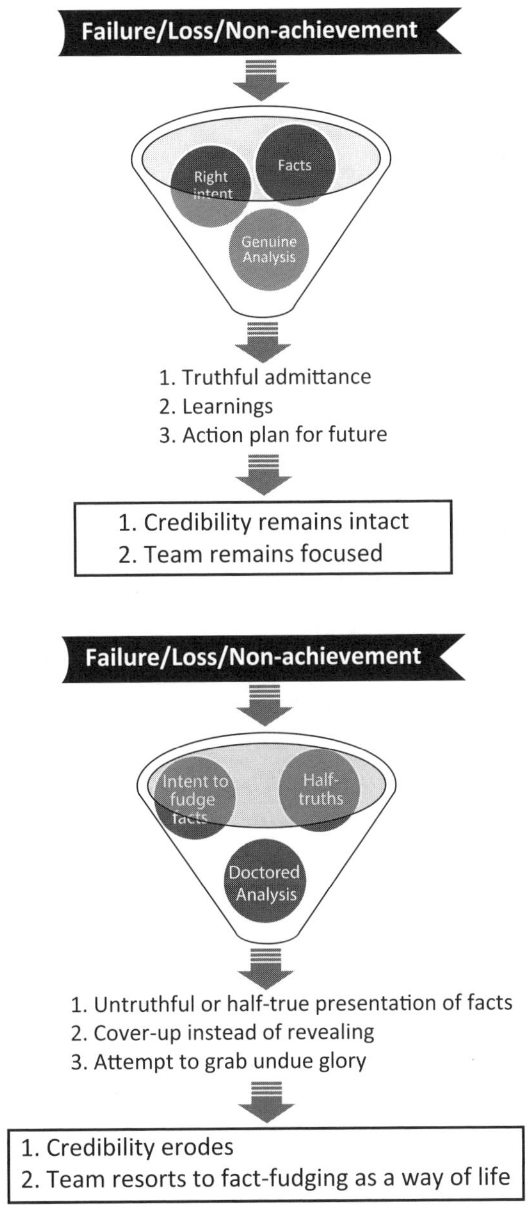

FIGURE 3: **Truth vs Half-Truth**

Key Takeaways

- If you are genuine in your efforts, diligent in your analysis, and upfront in admitting your mistakes, you can recover from any failure.
- Don't resort to window dressing when questioned for a misstep, a poor result, or failed effort. People can easily see through these tactics.
- You may think you outsmarted your audience by telling half-truths, but your credibility will soon erode.
- You will have infinite chances to bounce back from a bad performance, but it is nearly impossible to earn back people's trust in you or your team.
- Being clever can be useful during the planning and execution phases, but put that cleverness to rest when analysing your bad decisions or poor results.

Self-Evaluation

Reflect on how honest you are when presenting below-par performance, whether your own or that of your team members. Evaluate yourself with the following questions:

- Do you always present the facts as they are?
- Do you tend to glam up mediocre results by highlighting trivial achievements?
- Do you unjustifiably blame other teams or departments for your slip-ups?
- Do you believe in accepting failure with honesty?

Now, give yourself Credy Points based on your behaviour in the above context. Pick the appropriate option:

○ Always behave like a Credy: 10 Credy points

○ Mostly behave like a Credy: 7 Credy points

○ Sometimes behave like a Credy, sometimes like a Goofy: 4 Credy points

○ Always behave like a Goofy: 0 Credy points

'Mujhe joh sahi lagta hai mai karta hoon...
wo chahe bhagwan ke khilaaf ho,
samaaj ke khilaf ho, police, kanoon...
ya phir poore system ke khilaf kyun na ho.'

'Don ka intezaar toh baarah mulko ki police kar rahi hai,
but Don ko pakadna mushkil hi nahi, namumkin hai.'

4/36

Secure Credys versus Insecure Goofys

Have you ever seen someone raise their voice because their argument is weak? Or a colleague dominating his subordinates just to make them feel small? Have you had a colleague who is under constant pressure to prove that he's worthy of the position he has been given? These are all typical traits of someone who is low on confidence, doesn't have the right skills for the work he is doing, and wants to cling to his title or designation – in short, a very insecure Goofy. Insecure leaders are bad decision-makers. They behave irrationally, chase the wrong motives, and deliver poor results. Worse, they pass on their insecurity to their team members. No wonder, teams led by insecure Goofys are always underperforming and caught up in inconsequential issues.

The future is uncertain for all of us, and this is equally true for leaders. But insecure leaders who have never worked on their fundamentals live in constant fear of the unknown. Their lack of knowledge and skills – and hence their poor self-belief – throws them into a vicious cycle of acting insanely and sabotaging their credibility.

In contrast, leaders who have a strong core, solid fundamentals, and the right intentions don't get bogged down by uncertainty. They have confidence in their abilities, and that alone makes them secure. These leaders don't crumble under pressure. Instead, they overpower their fears and take control of affairs without losing composure. Taking one step at a time, they use their knowledge, skills, and experience to find solutions. They have done it in the past, and they know they can do it again. As a result, they command a natural liking, loyalty, and respect from others.

Goofys, unfortunately, succumb to pressure from day one. Easily overwhelmed by everyday hiccups and challenges, they lose all control. Their poor fundamentals and weak intent reflect in their behaviour. They are constantly haunted by a complex because, deep down, they know that they are not leadership material. And since they fail to command respect, they stoop to a level where they have to demand it.

Let me share an example of both types of leaders, starting with a Credy leader I had back in the day. One morning, he called me to his cabin for a feedback session. The discussion that followed is a classic example of how secure leaders behave and how they treat others.

He started by saying that I was doing great work, then added that it was time for me to get over my shyness and start claiming credit for my efforts. Being a backstage-loving guy, I had never been comfortable talking about my achievements. However, my leader explained that this was depriving me of the recognition I deserved and, because I was stage shy, he was the one getting most of the face time and limelight. Here, 'stage' refers to the forums and events where people are recognised for their work.

Now, an insecure leader might never have brought this up. But this Credy wanted his team members to get their fair share of applause and glory. With his encouragement, I started going on stage occasionally to make a presentation or accept an award on behalf of my team.

While I got the recognition, I also learned an important lesson: Credy leaders know how to overcome their insecurities, and they are not afraid to let their team members enjoy the spotlight.

Conversely, a Goofy leader I worked with had the most fragile ego. He was always on a hunt for anything he saw as an insult to him, but he was particularly judgemental, secretive, and rude with his juniors.

Since he had neither the intent nor the content to be a good leader, he was often ridiculed by his peers and seniors. This further fuelled his bad behaviour, and instead of working on his competencies, he chose to supress his team members at every single opportunity. Basically, he was brutally insecure, and this drove all his decisions and actions.

Once, while on our way back from a meeting with a franchise, this Goofy started asking me random questions about the territory I was handling. I was surprised by his line of questioning, but more surprised by his fault-finding tone. It felt like he was trying to corner me on any issue he could find. Only later in the conversation did I realise what was going on, when he revealed the real reason he was upset.

At the franchise's office, after Goofy had addressed their team, I took over and sort of concluded the discussion. Apparently, this made him feel overshadowed because 'the podium' had been snatched from him. According to this demi-god, no one should speak after him so that his words were seen as full and final. But since he did not have the courage to say this to me directly, he decided to grill me about my territory and performance. However, being a typical Goofy, he could not control himself for too long and blurted out his true feelings.

After this incident, he turned into an even bigger Goofy in my eyes.

Sadly, leaders with poor self-esteem don't understand that their authority cannot be undermined by such trivial things. They have a larger canvas to paint, and that requires a big heart, an open mind, and loads of self-belief.

To summarise, if you feel insecure as a leader, my advice is to introspect and kill those demons of insecurity bothering you. More often than not, they are nothing but your imagination, though sometimes there may be an underlying personal issue that needs your attention.

I will even go to the extent of recommending a change of role, or even stepping down, rather than living with insecurity because you feel inferior to your colleagues. You want a leadership role where you can contribute, not where you feel the need to bulldoze others every day to feel good about yourself.

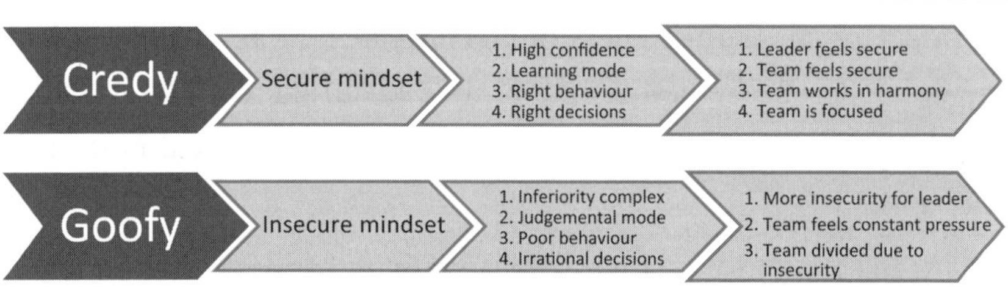

FIGURE 4: **Secure vs Insecure Mindset: Progression and Effect**

Key Takeaways

- Feeling threatened by your own team members is the worst you can do to yourself. Competing with them will only make you look bad even if you end up winning.
- Security or insecurity is a mindset, and it affects your behaviour as a leader. If you can correct your mindset, your behaviour with others will take care of itself.
- All leaders face rough times, but great leaders don't let it affect their self-belief. Take the time to introspect, and cultivate confidence in your abilities.
- Ultimately, your issues are your own and not your team's. Your personal or professional matters should not affect how you treat your team members.

Self-Evaluation

Reflect on how you handle feelings of insecurity and self-doubt as a leader. Evaluate yourself with the following questions:

- Do you feel threatened by your direct or indirect reportees?
- Do you knowingly use your position or title to dominate your colleagues or make them feel inferior?
- Are you able to make rational decisions even when you're feeling insecure?

Now, give yourself Credy Points based on your behaviour in the above context. Pick the appropriate option:

- ○ Always behave like a Credy: 10 Credy points
- ○ Mostly behave like a Credy: 7 Credy points
- ○ Sometimes behave like a Credy, sometimes like a Goofy: 4 Credy points
- ○ Always behave like a Goofy: 0 Credy points

Your vibe attracts your tribe.

5/36

Law of Attraction

YOU MAY HAVE seen two contrasting approaches when someone is building a team or creating an ecosystem of resources. First is the 'horses for courses' approach, which means selecting the best-fit person or entity for a role. Second is the 'flatterers first' approach, which means selecting yes-men regardless of their skills or competence for the job. In this context, the law of attraction means that leaders naturally attract – and choose – people who mirror their own work ethic, principles, and attitude towards work. Because, quite simply, your vibe attracts your tribe!

Whenever a leader is asked to recruit a new team member, vendor, supplier, partner, or service provider, his leadership qualities are unknowingly put to the test. In this case, too, Credys and Goofys handle the process in very different ways.

Credys invariably look for people who are a good fit for the organisation in terms of both competence and culture. They select candidates who can deliver results while adhering to the company's value system. Especially when hiring team members, they are not afraid to hire people who might be more knowledgeable or experienced than them in certain areas.

In other words, Credys are not threatened by talent. They know how to handle talent and how to nurture a good professional into a great performer.

Credys attract Credys and Goofys attract Goofys.

But this logical selection process is not followed by all leaders. Goofys, as you might expect, look for people who are a notch or two 'less' than them in terms of knowledge, skills, experience, and confidence. These leaders love being surrounded by gullible colleagues who cannot or will not question their decisions. In short, Goofys want worshippers, not performers, regardless of whether they are suited to the mission at hand.

These dramatically opposite selection processes have a direct and proportional impact on the results produced by people. While teams led by Credys, curated through a rational selection process, thrive and shine, those led by Goofys lag and stumble. While one becomes a formidable force in the organisation, the other ruins whatever good was achieved by its predecessors. I will illustrate this with two classic examples, starting with that of a Credy.

I once reported to a department head who had developed his own meticulous process of hiring new team members. In addition to an interview, candidates were tested through case studies and technical tasks related to the job. Each shortlisted profile was then dissected by my leader for its suitability to the role, cost to the company, and the candidate's expectations from the organisation.

What I truly admired about this Credy was that he never seemed threatened by people who knew more than him. For example, when we needed a department representative for our IT needs, he made it clear that we should look for an IT specialist and not a generalist – someone who could communicate our exact requirements to the IT department but could also fix minor issues on his own.

After a rigorous selection process, he selected someone who had extensive IT experience and a pedigree that was unmatched. During the final interview, the candidate corrected us on a few technical points. In this scenario, any ordinary leader would let his ego get the better of him and reject the candidate. But Credy appreciated the candidate's confidence and told him he was hired.

The decision paid off. Our new colleague proved to be an invaluable asset for the team, as having our own IT expert significantly reduced our lag times.

As a leader, you need a good amount of *Crediniyat* to digest the fact that a person junior to you in age and experience knows more than you and has the guts to correct you, and that too during an interview. My leader clearly had plenty of it. In fact, to this day he is known for his knack of hiring people with the right qualifications, a great track record, and a near-perfect cultural fit.

Goofys, being insecure, will never hire people who are more qualified or more experienced than them. In fact, one of my Goofy leaders had a simple hiring strategy: look for people who can be tamed easily.

In those days, we had engaged a vendor to train my team to work more efficiently. However, months passed and we did not see any significant improvements. So we found another vendor with better credentials and a lower cost to the company.

We asked the vendor for a proposal, and their presentation left us with no doubts whatsoever. They answered all our questions patiently and successfully. But they made one fatal mistake – they failed to oil our Goofy leader's ego during the presentation or in the follow-up meetings. In other words, they did not give him feelers that they would be his potential worshippers. As expected, Goofy rejected this vendor.

Being a conservative organisation, we could not question our leader beyond a point, but it was obvious why he did this. He wasn't looking for the best in business but for those who would treat him like a lord. As always, he was threatened by bright people and so he rejected them at the first opportunity.

Fortunately, his Goofy ways did not go unnoticed for long. Word soon reached the senior leadership, and the HR team was instructed to exclude him from all hiring decisions unless absolutely necessary.

By now, you must have understood how Goofys attract Goofys, creating a *Goofiland* around themselves but leaving the organisation vulnerable in the process. While Goofys chill in their short-lived fantasy world, Credys build an indestructible fort brick by brick, with strong team members and loyal collaborators. Credys know that they are only as strong as the collective strength of their immediate circle, so they are very selective about who they let into their *Crediverse*.

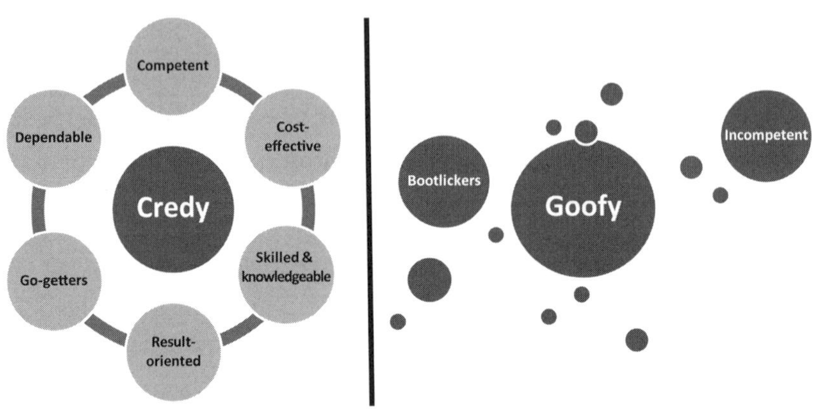

FIGURE 5: **Formidable Credy Team vs Feeble Goofy Team**

Key Takeaways

- Collecting minnows will not make you a leader. Instead, you will be seen as an insecure narcissist who wants colleagues that can be easily bullied.
- Accept that you don't know everything. There will always be colleagues who know more than you about certain subjects.
- When you select people based on suitability rather than flattery, you will be seen as a confident leader who can be trusted with bigger roles. You will be perceived as someone who can comfortably lead and manage stalwarts and subject matter experts.

Self-Evaluation

Reflect on how rational you are when selecting people or providers for a job. Evaluate yourself with the following questions:

- Is it fitment or flattery that governs your hiring decisions? In other words, do you choose the best people for the job or those who appear weak and submissive?
- Do you believe that you know everything about everything?
- Can you handle a team member or collaborator who has more knowledge than you in a specific area?
- Do you value the contributions of others to your accomplishments?

Now, give yourself Credy Points based on your behaviour in the above context. Pick the appropriate option:

- ○ Always behave like a Credy: 10 Credy points
- ○ Mostly behave like a Credy: 7 Credy points
- ○ Sometimes behave like a Credy, sometimes like a Goofy: 4 Credy points
- ○ Always behave like a Goofy: 0 Credy points

'Crime Master Gogo naam hai mera,
aankhen nikal ke gotiyan khelta hun main.'

6/36

Nostalgia Gone Wrong: Goofys Who Live in the Past

THINK OF LEADERS who constantly brag about their past or who constantly compare you to someone from their past – a person you don't even know – and they do this not in a flattering manner but to make you feel inferior. On the other hand, think of those who show an interest in you and your story and share their experience only when you are eager to learn from them. Who would you choose as your mentor?

People change jobs all the time. Sometimes, they change departments or move to a different location in the same organisation. With every move, they encounter a new ecosystem, with new people, processes, objectives, and legacies (what went right in the past and what didn't). It is, in many ways, a new beginning with its own opportunities and challenges that need a fresh perspective.

However, the physical move to a new role is not always accompanied by a mental move. While some leaders adapt quickly and use their knowledge and experience to thrive in the new role, others have a habit of clinging to the past. They use their past achievements to project a falsified grand image of themselves. This 'last organisation syndrome' is rampant among senior leaders

– a compulsive behaviour where the leader fails to detach from his past glories and make a fresh start.

The difference between Credys and Goofys lies in how they handle this transition. Let's talk about Goofys first. Goofys use their past to glorify themselves as leaders who never failed, who built perfect teams, and who were indispensable to their previous employers. In short, they portray themselves as superhumans who are a prized catch for any employer.

But this obsession with the past comes at a cost. The constant reminiscing and lamenting hurts the leader's image, alienates him from colleagues, and destroys the team's morale. Let me share how some Goofys end up achieving these three unwanted outcomes.

I had a Goofy project lead who loved living in the past. At every team meeting, he would start the discussion as usual, but within minutes he would get nostalgic about his previous job, quoting examples of how brilliantly he managed a similar agenda in that role. Oblivious to our discomfort, he would rave about his ex-employer's policies and processes and the great colleagues he had there. And he never forgot to mention how much he was admired there and how badly he was being missed.

In his view, waxing eloquence about his past was a smart move meant to inspire us. But it had just the opposite effect. Instead of motivating us to outdo his ex-colleagues, it left us feeling that he was unhappy being our leader and saw us as mediocre performers. The harder we tried to prove ourselves, the more his tall claims from the past pulled us down. On most days, he acted like a guest leader who had taken time off from his so-called 'dream team' to come and work with us.

Throughout this Goofy's tenure, we were under constant pressure to meet his expectations, but with no first-hand experience of his past heroics, we could never replicate those glories for him. The net outcome of this tug of war was a big negative.

When we couldn't take it anymore, we decided to cross-check Goofy's tall claims. We had always suspected his stories were nothing but Goofy tales, but we had to be sure. Unsurprisingly, we found that he had been quite an average leader who was almost kicked out of his last organisation owing to his numerous Goofy traits.

On the flip side, I've seen many Credy leaders handle their transition exceptionally well. One Credy particularly comes to mind. He joined us from a reputed rival brand that was doing far better than us, and he came with an illustrious resume and an impeccable reputation. We were in awe the moment we learned he would be leading our team.

Our company was not doing well at the time, and this leader was seen as a turnaround guy who could save us from a potential shutdown. In such a position, any leader would be tempted to abuse his authority and question everyone and everything. But this Credy was built of different stuff. He came, he joined, and he took the time to learn about us as a team and a company. Our processes, our challenges and strategies, he reviewed everything.

He took a few good weeks to replace his learner's cap with a leader's cap. Forget boasting about his past, if he had a noteworthy experience to share, he would pick his words with utmost care, starting with expressions like 'In my experience…' or 'My experience says…' The best part was that he never, ever took names or mentioned specific details, and yet he always managed to make his point. Clearly, his intention was to share his learnings and not to belittle us.

This Credy also used another expression quite generously: 'I will be happy to be proved wrong.' It was his way of telling us that even if a particular strategy had not worked for us in the past, he was ready to take the risk and see if we could pull it through a second time.

Under his leadership, the business started to flourish and we soon climbed out of the sinkhole of constant losses.

There is no debate about the benefits of applying your experience to a new role, but using your past successes to berate your current team is useless at best and harmful at worst. More often than not, adopting a cut-copy-paste strategy from your past will fall on its face. Instead, take the time to learn about your new team's journey so far, and then come up with solutions that will work for their unique circumstances.

For example, let's say you previously led a team that designed ad campaigns for luxury cars, but your current team designs ads for entry-level cars. This changes everything, including the target customer, the message, design elements, choice of media, ad frequency, and so on. So you need to guide your team accordingly. Your earlier strategies may not work here, but your knowledge of designing ad campaigns will still be an asset.

In sum, I am not discouraging you from applying your learnings to your current role. I'm only suggesting that you do it subtly. Use logical arguments rather than anecdotes to convince and motivate your people!

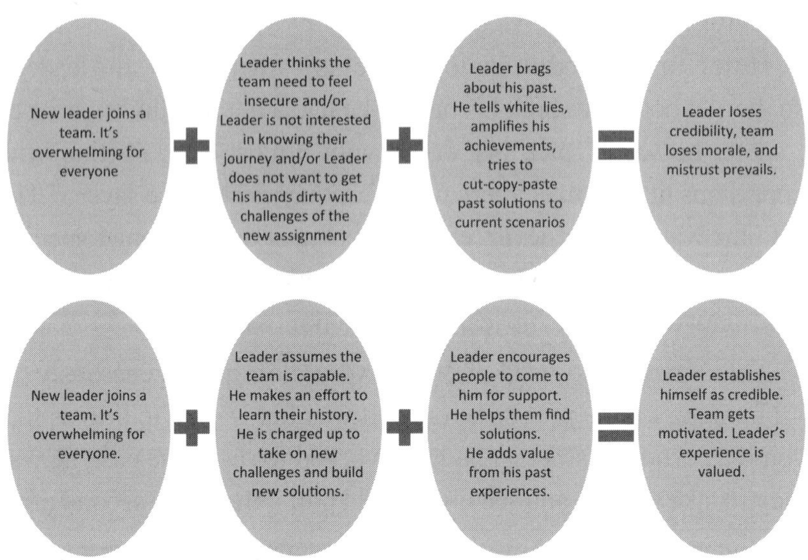

FIGURE 6: **Boisterous Bragging vs Modest Humility**

Key Takeaways

- Bury it! Yes, bury the nostalgia of your past organisations, colleagues, and successes if you want to make a mark in your new workplace.
- Frankly, no one wants to hear endless stories of greatness about your previous teams. The more you compare, the unhappier you will be and the more unhappiness you will spread. Resist the temptation of ruminating about the past, and avoid citing experiences that will demotivate your current team.
- Prudence in what you share from your past and how you share it will define you as a Credy or a Goofy.

Self-Evaluation

Reflect on whether you have a tendency to brag about your past. Evaluate yourself with the following questions:

- Do you boast about your past successes to show that you are superior to others?
- Can you share your learnings in a way that doesn't make others feel like non-achievers?
- Do you appreciate that every new job role brings unique opportunities and challenges that need a new approach?
- Do you think it's important to understand your new team (their history, opportunities, challenges faced, initiatives taken) before you start throwing solutions at them from your past?

Now, give yourself Credy Points based on your behaviour in the above context. Pick the appropriate option:

- ○ Always behave like a Credy: 10 Credy points
- ○ Mostly behave like a Credy: 7 Credy points
- ○ Sometimes behave like a Credy, sometimes like a Goofy: 4 Credy points
- ○ Always behave like a Goofy: 0 Credy points

'Wo jaisa bhi hai mera putr hai.'

7/36

The Fine Line between Having Favourites and Practising Favouritism

How would you feel about a sports coach who gives performance-enhancing tips to his favourites but ignores even the more talented players? What about a CEO who promotes an incompetent friend to head a key function, or a political leader who favours only a few sections of society? Definitely, you wouldn't think highly of these individuals. The fact remains that leaders, like anyone else, will always have a few favourites. But what distinguishes a Credy from a Goofy is what governs their decisions – objectivity or favouritism. While Credism is about making objective and fair choices, Goofism is about indiscriminately favouring one's favourites. Here, by 'favourites' I mean people a leader simply likes and feels comfortable with – not because of their competencies or contributions, but for their personality traits.

All leaders have their favourites, but the difference lies in how those relationships influence their day-to-day decisions. While Credys put the organisation's interests above personal preferences, Goofys make biased decisions that benefit their favourites, ignoring what is best for the organisation.

During one of my stints, I wasn't one of my Credy leader's favourites. That doesn't mean I was in his bad books, but we didn't share the rapport he had with some of my colleagues. This never deterred me from doing my best, but there was one particular year when, despite all my efforts, my performance dropped quite a bit.

With the annual performance review around the corner, I had every reason to believe I was going to get a low rating, especially since I wasn't a favourite. I walked into the review meeting braced for a rough ride, with no idea that a lesson in fine leadership was waiting for me.

To my surprise, my leader strongly defended my performance. He explained to the review team the personal and professional difficulties I had faced that year and the efforts I had put in to meet my targets despite those setbacks. Contrary to my apprehensions, he was extremely objective throughout the appraisal process. I received an 'Excellent' rating that year.

It was reassuring to see my hard work and dedication recognised by my leader even though we did not share a close relationship. And he displayed the same objectivity when evaluating his favourites, some of whom had shown impressive results but under very easy circumstances.

Without hesitation, he pointed out the conducive terrain they had available to them, adding that their performance was, in fact, not good enough and they could have done much better. Quite rightly, 'goodlooking' results when seen in light of circumstances were termed pretty average by a Credy leader who played tennis on weekends with these very colleagues.

This approach taken by my leader had a team-wide impact. Through his actions rather than words, he made it known that work meant work. No one was allowed to take things for granted, and poor results would be questioned regardless of how much he liked you.

Even in day-to-day matters like assigning routine tasks, allocating additional workload, or nominating us for a foreign trip or prestigious seminar, he was never partial. We never felt any pressure to be part of his inner circle to get privileged treatment; everyone was expected to work hard to earn the rewards. This kind of objectivity is rare, but it does exist.

It is thanks to this Credy that I learned the difference between having favourites and practising favouritism. There is nothing wrong with having a few colleagues that you like or admire more than others, as long as no one feels excluded or sidelined.

I have also worked with several Goofys of varying degrees who are openly biased towards some people. Their decisions and actions are based more on *whom* they wish to benefit rather than *what* needs to be done. As a result, their chosen ones receive preferential treatment regardless of their abilities, attitude, intent, or performance.

I had a Goofy leader who would assign the easiest tasks to his favourites and then give them excellent performance ratings. His decision-making compass was guided not by facts and figures but by the needs and wants of those he wanted to favour. For instance, there was no connection between the sales targets given to people and the sales promotion budgets allotted to them. The favourites got smaller targets and big promotional budgets, even though they faced no tough market conditions. They were also given easy dealers to manage. It was always an uneven playing field. And Goofy's *Goofaniyat* did not stop at this. He preferred to visit his favourites' dealers regardless of the need of the market.

Funnily, this Goofy was partial even in matters like where his blue-eyed boys sat in the bay, whose leave got approved or denied, and who had to work late while others left on time.

In the end, this objectivity-deprived favouritism severely affected our performance as a team. It also crushed our morale. Goofy's unequal and unjustified distribution of duties, authority, and rewards practically divided the team into haves and have-nots. Eventually, many of my talented and hardworking colleagues left the organisation. With the team now reduced to a few sycophants and their Goofy leader, I too left after some time.

In my experience, Goofys succumb to favouritism to satisfy their compulsive need to be surrounded by brown-nosers. The ability to resist this temptation is what sets Credys apart. Credys know that without integrity and fairness, they cannot build trust. They ensure the team knows that their decisions will never be coloured by personal choices. This is sacrosanct and non-negotiable in *Crediverse*.

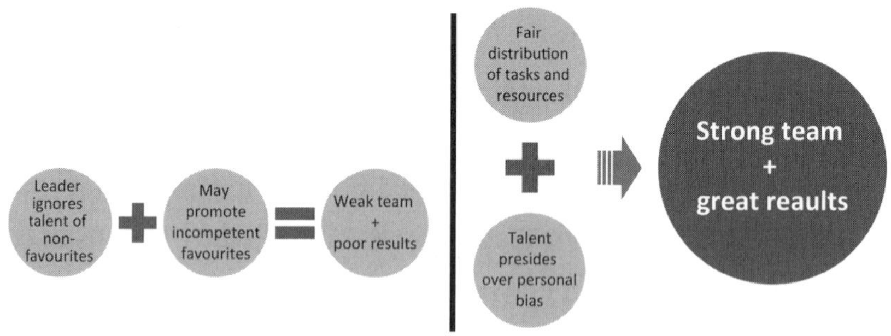

FIGURE 7: **Goofism vs Credism**

Key Takeaways

- Practising favouritism is a type of corruption in itself, where you create a coterie and use the organisation for your personal agendas rather than to grow the business.
- To be respected as a leader, you should be equally demanding of all your team members and ensure that resources are distributed adequately and fairly.

- Be a rational decision-maker. Specifically, decisions that can make or break careers, like performance ratings, promotions, and transfers, should never be compromised.
- Being just and objective is not just a must-have Credy trait; it is your duty to your profession and your organisation.
- Your time is an invaluable resource for your team. Be fair when allocating your time and avoid the temptation to spend more time with your favourites.
- Learn to work in harmony with competent people, even if they don't fit your definition of a likeable person.

Self-Evaluation

Reflect on how unbiased you are as a leader. Evaluate yourself with the following questions:

- Are you objective and impartial in your decisions and actions?
- Do you make the effort to appreciate and support team members who are not your favourites?
- Do you have the guts to show the mirror to your favourites when they are at fault?

Now, give yourself Credy Points based on your behaviour in the above context. Pick the appropriate option:

- ○ Always behave like a Credy: 10 Credy points
- ○ Mostly behave like a Credy: 7 Credy points
- ○ Sometimes behave like a Credy, sometimes like a Goofy: 4 Credy points
- ○ Always behave like a Goofy: 0 Credy points

'Logon ko haque jamana aata hai rishta nibhana nahi.'

8/36

Breaking Protocol the Right Way

EVERY ORGANISATION HAS certain protocols in place to ensure smooth workflow and harmony between teams and departments. These protocols are not always perfect and can definitely be bettered. One such unstated rule in almost every organisation is the expectation to follow the hierarchy when relaying information or taking an action. Though well-intentioned, this practice can hinder productivity and efficiency. Credible leaders respect hierarchical structures, but if the situation demands, they don't hesitate to bypass the chain of command. If there's a fire and you have the means to put it out, would you still wait for the fire brigade to arrive? I believe not! Remember, what works becomes the norm, and what is effective becomes protocol. What's important is to have a clear purpose and a proper method of sidestepping accepted procedures.

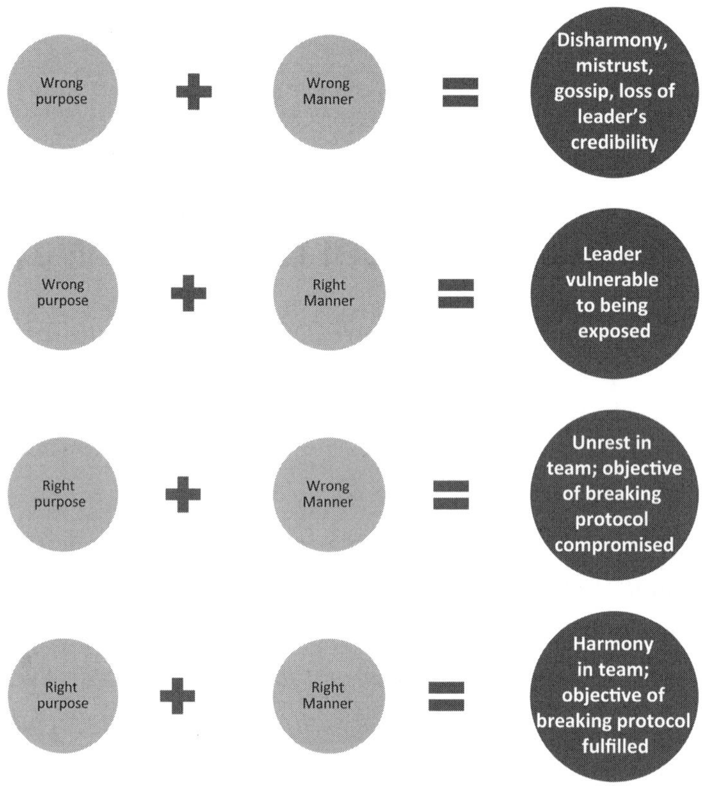

FIGURE 8a: **Breaking Protocol: Impact of Various Combinations of Purpose and Manner**

In organisations, hierarchies exist for a reason – to enable the smooth flow of information and actions. Everyone has a specific role to play, with an appropriate level of authority and responsibility. Even when this chain of command is not hardwired or imposed as a rule, it is expected to be followed without question. But sometimes, hierarchies need to be sidestepped.

Let's take the example of a three-tier hierarchy: a team, their leader, and a senior leader to whom the leader reports. At times, the senior leader may bypass his direct reportee and engage directly with the team. The righteousness of this skip-level interaction depends on two key factors: whether there is a need for the interaction (purpose) and the way it is conducted (manner).

As expected, Goofys goof up at the purpose stage itself, but the manner in which they execute skip interactions is even more intriguing. The outcome is doubtful and poisoned minds. Let me share an example.

One of my leaders, who was known more for his insinuations than any other quality, had a peculiar habit of calling my subordinates over the weekend just to ask random questions like what was going on in the office, how this person or that person was doing, who was favouring whom, what the latest news was, and so on. In short, he was looking for some *masala*, or 'juicy tales' as I call them. Even when my colleagues tried to dodge his questions, this Goofy would keep probing until he managed to extract some little detail that he could use as a secret weapon to corner me or another leader in the future. Even worse, he would ask my team members not to mention these conversations to anyone, although in most cases I ended up knowing them word by word.

Sadly, this Goofy was more interested in discussing people rather than the ideas or challenges that needed his attention. It was always about petty office politics and manipulating perceptions to his advantage. Another one of his trademark Goofy traits was to bypass me entirely and communicate key project details directly to my team members, which sent out a clear message that he and I were not aligned. This led to unnecessary rumour-mongering and created tension and disorder in my team. Some team members naturally took advantage of the situation, while others were left utterly confused.

As you can see, in this case, not only was the purpose of this Goofy's interactions questionable, but the manner in which they were carried out was also unethical.

While Credys, too, break the chain of command at times, they generally have a strong reason for it. More importantly, they execute skip-level interactions in a manner that doesn't cause discord.

I once reported to a Credy who never bypassed me unless it was absolutely necessary. When he did speak directly with my team members, he had a clear reason – to get first-hand information, share feedback on a report or project, or seek their opinion on an idea. On occasion, he had to do it because I was unavailable, or because going through me would have caused a fatal delay. In short, his skip-level interactions had a clear purpose.

The way my leader went about these interactions was also a lesson in itself. To start with, he always informed me in advance whom he would be speaking to and why. There were times when he needed to address a grievance directly or hold a one-on-one meeting without me to maintain confidentiality (especially when the issue was personal to the team member). But this was also done after taking me into confidence. He also made it a point to ask the individual to update me afterwards.

Did my leader need to do this? No. Did it make him any less of a leader? Absolutely not. On the contrary, his stature only grew in my eyes.

Because of this supreme level of transparency practised by my leader, we shared a fantastic working relationship. On the rare occasions when he met my team without informing me first, I never felt insecure or suspicious of his intentions.

I knew he had no hidden agenda and there was complete trust between us.

Of course, it is not always possible to maintain this level of transparency, especially when the greater good of the organisation is at stake. For instance, if someone is being investigated for integrity issues and their leader is tasked with getting the truth out, he may need to bypass all hierarchies to extract the facts. In this case, the leader cannot be blamed for breaking protocol. Confidentiality is paramount here, and therefore transparency will take a backseat.

Whatever the situation, the key is to be a Credy in your intent and actions. Break hierarches and protocols if needed, but never break trust!

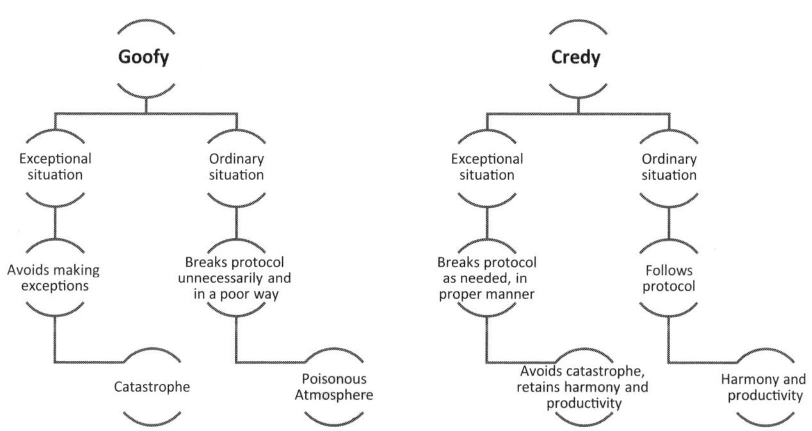

FIGURE 8b: **Ill-willed Goofy vs Righteous Credy**

Key Takeaways

- While standard operating procedures apply to standard workflows and typical situations, exceptional circumstances demand exceptional behaviour and unprecedented actions.
- If you must bypass hierarchy, have a clear purpose, do it in the right manner, and be transparent in your communication.
- As a leader, it is your responsibility to redefine established rules based on your learnings.
- When breaking a protocol, remember to apply the ideal combination of right purpose and right manner.
- Build protocols that enhance productivity and not create obstacles.

Self-Evaluation

Reflect on your approach to protocols as a leader. Evaluate yourself with the following questions:

- Are you able to break away from standard procedures when necessary?
- Do you understand that mere good intention is not sufficient; the right approach is necessary when dealing across hierarchies?
- Do you bypass protocol in a way that helps the greater cause without harming anyone?
- Do you inform all concerned parties before taking an exceptional action?
- Do you understand that bypassing your reportees without their knowledge can cause insecurity and mistrust?

Now, give yourself Credy Points based on your behaviour in the above context. Pick the appropriate option:

- ○ Always behave like a Credy: 10 Credy points
- ○ Mostly behave like a Credy: 7 Credy points
- ○ Sometimes behave like a Credy, sometimes like a Goofy: 4 Credy points
- ○ Always behave like a Goofy: 0 Credy points

'Jaa Simran jaa, ji le apni zindagi!'

9/36

Easy Exits

SOME LEADERS FORGET that the people they are leading are free human beings, not their lifelong slaves. These humans each have their own emotions, aspirations, likes, and dislikes that motivate them to grow personally and professionally. In pursuit of this growth, some of them will inevitably move on to better opportunities. Generally, it is a move that benefits the individual but creates challenges for the leader. Besides disrupting the workflow, it tests the leader in terms of how he handles the exit and, more importantly, how easy or difficult he makes the exit process for the outgoing team member.

Let's acknowledge a harsh reality that's true for any organisation – people don't get growth opportunities very often. Moreover, very few are lucky enough to get a role that aligns with their interests and aspirations. So, at any given time, a significant number of employees are looking out for change.

Every exit disturbs the workflow for a while, but things eventually get back to normal. This is where a leader's role becomes critical. Despite the jolt, he has to keep his team on track and the results under control.

I have witnessed many exits in my professional life, but there were two occasions where the respective leaders handled the departures in completely different ways. Their contrasting approaches revealed a lot about the right and wrong ways to handle such situations. Let's see what happened.

We have all heard horror stories of leaders who give a real hard time to their outgoing subordinates. These Goofys see people not as professionals but as their personal slaves. I once worked with a leader who created a big ruckus when anyone in our team resigned. On one occasion, he went to the extent of calling a colleague a 'traitor' in a room full of people. There was no secret project this person was handling, nor had he taken an oath that he would never leave the company; it was simply a case of getting a better opportunity elsewhere. But our Goofy leader couldn't take it. 'How can he leave when I gave him such a high performance rating last year?' he complained.

To get even, this Goofy forced a full three-month notice period on the poor fellow. With no work assigned to him, he would come to the office and sit idle all day.

No one gained anything here, except our leader, who seemed to get sadistic pleasure from our colleague's suffering. And who lost? The employee, definitely, who had to suffer for three months just to satisfy this Goofy's ego. In the end, he didn't even get a farewell and left feeling bitter and hurt. Thanks to our leader's goofiness, the bridge between them was burned forever.

The biggest loser, however, was the organisation, which paid full salary to a disengaged employee who was making zero contribution to the business. The company's image also took a beating, as my colleague later shared his experience with dozens of people in the industry. I'm sure this would have dissuaded many from joining the organisation.

This is how, in the hands of a Goofy leader, the exit process becomes unnecessarily dramatic and painful. Unfortunately, our Goofy leader learned nothing from the experience. Every subsequent exit in the team was equally unpleasant. Eventually, people found a way around it. To escape his wrath, they would send in their resignation and then go on medical leave, or simply not turn up for the next few days. Multiple complaints were raised against this Goofy, emails were sent to the managing director, but nothing much came of it.

At any rate, this incident revealed his true colours to us. We now knew how he treated his outgoing subordinates – the same people he called 'family members' up until the day they resigned.

On the positive side, I've also seen quite a few graceful exits under Credy leaders. Once, when a colleague resigned, our Credy leader had a heart-to-heart conversation with him to understand his reasons and see if he could be retained. When it was clear that he was determined to leave, our leader promised to make the exit process as smooth and structured as possible. His work was quickly reassigned to another team member, and a notice period was set based on the time required for the handover.

Because of the support he received in making a smooth and graceful exit, my colleague worked exceptionally hard during his final days with the company. He was given a befitting farewell, and he left with dignity, good memories, and lifelong admiration for our leader.

In this case, everyone was a winner – the outgoing employee, the team member who took his place, the rest of the team, our leader, and, of course, the organisation. This experience turned me into a devoted follower of my Credy leader.

Some Credys go even a step further. Using their knowledge of the outgoing employee's capabilities and work style, they guide him on how to succeed in his new role and the pitfalls to avoid. These leaders are true mentors and smooth operators who know how to treat people the right way. And their good deeds don't go unrequited. Many of their ex-team members return the good karma in their own ways. For instance, my Credy leader from the above story had a solid network in the industry, thanks in part to his former team members working in different organisations.

Of course, this is an ideal scenario. In reality, many leaders fail to separate their personal feelings from their professional and moral responsibility towards an exiting employee. They forget that people are free to choose what benefits them most. But more importantly, they forget that the way they handle an exit reveals a lot about their own true nature, as well as their ability to manage disruptions and keep the rest of the team motivated.

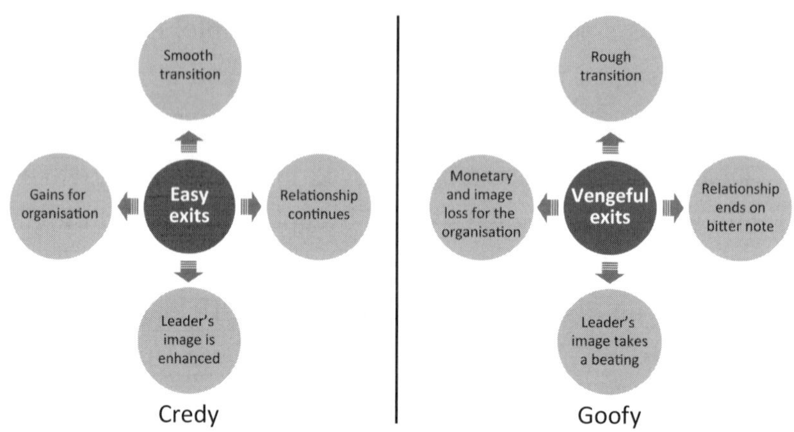

FIGURE 9: **Contrasting Approach – Contrasting Outcomes**

Key Takeaways

- People leave an organisation either because they have found something better or because they feel compelled to leave. There is no point in begging, pestering, or enticing them to stay. Instead, invest your energy in ensuring a smooth handover to the next incumbent.
- Making life miserable for an outgoing team member only makes your own life difficult. You lose loyalty and respect and, ultimately, your credibility.
- When an exit is inevitable, do your best to make it memorable (unless it is on grounds of integrity, indiscipline, or other such concern). This is a time to build bridges, not burn them forever.

Self-Evaluation

Reflect on how gracefully you handle exits as a leader. Evaluate yourself with the following questions:

- Do you accept that each of your team members, no matter how happy they seem today, may leave one day?
- Do you trust yourself to set aside your ego and ensure a smooth exit when a team member resigns?
- Do you believe in maintaining long-term relationships with your colleagues even after they have moved on?

Now, give yourself Credy Points based on your behaviour in the above context. Pick the appropriate option:

- ○ Always behave like a Credy: 10 Credy points
- ○ Mostly behave like a Credy: 7 Credy points
- ○ Sometimes behave like a Credy, sometimes like a Goofy: 4 Credy points
- ○ Always behave like a Goofy: 0 Credy points

CHAMPIONS

10/36

Shared Triumphs

HOW WOULD YOU feel about a leader who comes for a victory speech after a sports match, an election win, or a team performance, but harps on only about himself without mentioning anyone else? In contrast, what would you make of a leader who puts the spotlight on his teammates instead and talks at length about their contributions? I'm sure your thoughts about these two personalities would be poles apart. On one side is selfishness, on the other, humility. One side is repulsive, the other attractive. One side is Goofism, the other, Credism.

In moments of success, a leader's credibility can rise or fall dramatically, laying bare his true character as either an inspiring figure or a demoralising narcissist.

Credy leaders believe in sharing credit for their successes. They are aware of their own role in the win, but they never lose sight of the fact that it was a collective effort. At felicitation events, rather than celebrating their own individual brilliance, they make it a point to highlight their team's efforts. Goofy leaders, as you might expect, try to steal the limelight at every opportunity. Forget about giving credit where it's due, they shamelessly lay claim to achievements that are not even their own. This selfish behaviour pushes them further into the Goofy zone.

One of my Credy leaders was a tough taskmaster who constantly pushed us to get better at our work. Under his leadership, we achieved many unprecedented milestones. What made my tenure with him even more special was the way he credited our achievements. There were two aspects to his approach: first, he would ensure that the glorification happened before a large audience, where he applauded our efforts loud and clear and not just for the sake of it. Second, he acknowledged the individual contribution of each team member, as well as everyone else who supported our mission.

For as long as I worked with this Credy, never once did I see him try to hog the limelight. He belonged to a different league altogether.

When he was wrong, he admitted it without hesitation. During some performance cycles, if a decision of his backfired and we missed our target, he would openly talk about it at meetings, recognition events, and other forums. He would describe the events right from where he went wrong and how the team worked hard to correct the situation. At times, when he had doubts about our ability to meet a target or complete a project and we proved him wrong, he wasn't embarrassed to acknowledge it to the relevant audience.

Due to his consistent and sincere recognition of our work, the blood, sweat, and tears we shed under this taskmaster never bothered us. His humility and honesty magnified our team's glory, and it certainly amplified his credibility among one and all. People dreamed of working with him.

My other example comes from a Goofy who led another team in the same organisation. His habit to snatch credit was so obvious that people had nicknamed him 'Mr I, me, myself'. Badmouthing his own team members was a favourite pastime of this Goofy. According to him, they were 'just a bunch of useless junkies' who knew nothing.

But as they say, what goes around comes around. We had a town hall meeting, where this Goofy once again tried to capitalise on a team achievement as his personal triumph. But then came the boomerang. Someone from the audience asked him to explain how the superlative results were achieved. Goofy being Goofy was caught off guard and had to sheepishly call one of his team members on stage to explain the strategy behind the success.

Sometimes Goofys get exposed like this, although it's a different story that this particular Goofy did not stop his credit-snatching behaviour even after embarrassing himself at a public forum.

Naturally, the morale of this Goofy's team was always in pieces. They knew they would never get credit for their work, as their leader wanted to see his name and only his name on the plaque of success. His *Goofaniyat* was so apparent that, out of both sympathy and appreciation, other leaders made it a point to congratulate his team directly on their achievements. His team members often confided that they felt more like bonded labourers than valuable contributors to the organisation.

The fact is, success can be intoxicating. In moments of glory, even the best leaders can get carried away and try to claim a collective achievement as their own. They forget that it is always a symphony and never a solo show. In the end, it all comes down to how secure you are as a person. Insecure leaders fall for a moment of fame, but the secure ones set a precedent by letting others take centre stage. Ultimately, this is what decides whether you will be remembered as a generous socialist or a self-centred egomaniac when it comes to sharing credit.

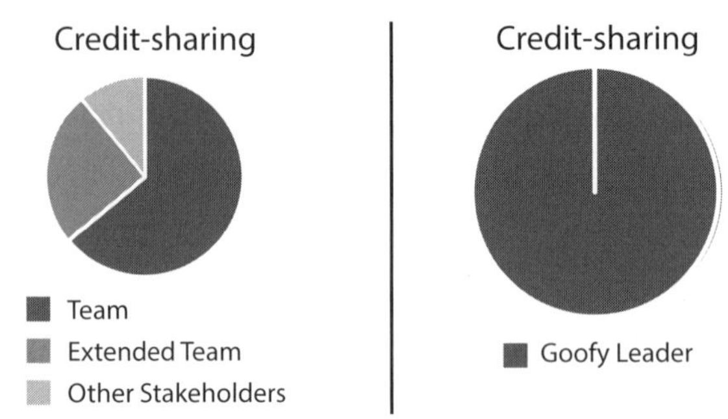

FIGURE 10: **Credism vs Goofism**

Key Takeaways

- Have the heart of a Credy leader: praise without fear. Have the eyes of a Credy leader: notice the efforts of your people. Have the fortitude of a Credy leader: publicly acknowledge those who stood behind you in your mission.
- Be the last in line to claim the trophy and the first to acknowledge those who helped you win it. In the end, how you handle the narrative after a win will decide the morale of your team, who are expected to soon start chasing a new milestone.
- Stealing credit may satisfy your ego momentarily, but you will lose the trust and support of your team. A leader is supposed to shine along with his team and not bury them under his shadow.
- If you are competing with your own team members, take it as a sign to introspect and ask yourself some hard questions.

Self-Evaluation

Reflect on how large-hearted you are when it comes to recognising the contributions of others to your successes. Evaluate yourself with the following questions:

- Do you acknowledge and appreciate the efforts of your team members?
- Do you share credit for success with your team?
- Do you extend genuine gratitude to stakeholders beyond your team who helped you succeed?

Now, give yourself Credy Points based on your behaviour in the above context. Pick the appropriate option:

- ○ Always behave like a Credy: 10 Credy points
- ○ Mostly behave like a Credy: 7 Credy points
- ○ Sometimes behave like a Credy, sometimes like a Goofy: 4 Credy points
- ○ Always behave like a Goofy: 0 Credy points

Protector

*'Kamaal is baat ka nahin hai Shekhar ki usne wo zameen khali karwa di ya 5 lakh rupay ka intezaam itni jaldi karliya ...
kamaal ye hai ki wo janta tha ki wo ye sab kuch kar sakta tha...'*

'Ye aadmi zindagi me kuch na kuch karega...'

11/36

From Praise to Power: Turning Foes into Allies

YOU MIGHT HAVE the strongest team in the organisation, but it cannot thrive unless it knows how to get cooperation and collaboration from others. Your strengths get multiplied and your weaknesses get cover fire if those outside your team willingly support your team members. To this effect, how you deal with collaborators and competitors within the organisation directly impacts the kind of cooperation your team will receive. A sure-fire way to create allies out of competing coworkers is by genuinely acknowledging the good work of others and sharing credit where due. In other words, to help your team succeed, you must act as their goodwill ambassador at all times.

Anyone who is a part of the corporate world knows that it is a jungle out there, where resources and opportunities are limited, where loss for one is gain for another, and where ambition rules over trust. Darwin's theory of survival of the fittest is fully applicable in this world, and with this as the base assumption, every leader finds himself in an 'us versus them' situation even within his own organisation.

That's fair enough, but does it mean a leader should not try to create allies? Certainly not! In fact, that is what Credy leaders do – they consciously and purposefully cultivate both internal and external allies, because they know what the absence of allies can mean for their team. As history has taught us, countries with peaceful borders and cooperative neighbours thrive better than those constantly facing hostilities within and without their borders.

While it takes many small actions, positive habits, and consistent effort to build internal allies, one time-tested approach is to recognise the accomplishments of your rival teams. Through honest appreciation, those vying for the same pie of the budget, position, or power can be turned into genuine supporters. This simple practice, although rarely followed, can make it easier for your team to navigate the organisational jigsaw.

I learned the value of applauding others' work from a Credy leader who was a natural at making allies. He had his share of ideological differences with his peers, there were disagreements over common issues, and the environment was rife with egos and intense competition. Yet he never hesitated to commend the achievements of his rivals.

He was also very selective with his words of appreciation – always sincere and authentic and never ingratiating. Not just this, he openly praised worthy colleagues even in their absence. If he noticed something good in another team, he made it a point to tell us about it.

This approach of our Credy leader had a multifold effect on us. It added to our knowledge, kept us competitive, and created a camaraderie with our rival teams that was unheard of before. Above all, it taught us to see value in the work of others. We started to feel like we were a part of the bigger successes of the organisation, at times only as enthusiastic spectators, but never as envying coworkers.

Such positive behaviour from a leader breaks barriers and builds synergies that benefit everyone. Thanks to our leader's efforts, whenever we found ourselves presenting to a room full of people with different motives (remember Darwin's theory?), we had many allies in the audience.

Appreciation is generally infectious. As a reciprocation of our leader's efforts, we too started receiving recognition for achievements that might not have generated an ounce of enthusiasm otherwise. And this was not limited to presentations or town halls. Whenever we requested extra support from other teams that was over and above the norm – be it a quicker response, access to data, or an expert opinion – we got it. While each of us played our part to maintain this atmosphere of harmony and collaboration, it was our leader who led from the front.

In contrast to Credy leaders, Goofys at best keep mum when a rival team is recognised for its work. I once had a colleague, aptly nicknamed 'Mr Faultfinder', who categorically started and ended every conversation with a critical comment about other leaders or their teams. He loved finding faults and mocking others behind their backs.

For instance, if a team surpassed its targets, he would trivialise their success by saying, 'They were just lucky. If the conditions for sales had not been so conducive, they would never have hit those numbers.' Or he would say, 'So what if they met their target. I've done that plenty of times!' More often than not, such remarks were followed by a boring monologue about his own achievements.

On the rare occasion when this Goofy did utter a word of appreciation, his body language, gestures, tone, and choice of words appeared so forced and synthetic that anyone could see how jealous and critical he was feeling inside.

His attitude obviously strained relationships, but it was even more detrimental for his own team. They lost an important support system in the organisation and were given last priority when they needed cooperation from others. Worse still, they were constantly under attack from anyone who wanted to get back at their Goofy leader.

Of course, his low-level talks also wasted everyone's time. There were some who pretended to be interested in his conversations, but eventually those yes-men also started showing signs of goofiness. Misplaced loyalty landed some of my brightest colleagues in the mediocre cadre for good.

This is what Goofy leaders do. Instead of acting as a roadblock-buster for their team, they become the biggest roadblocks themselves.

As a leader, it is your duty to break down the invisible walls between your team and the rest of the organisation. One of the easiest ways to do this is through sincere appreciation. It forces the guards down, masks are removed, and hands of collaboration are extended.

Unlike in physics, where opposites attract, here positivity attracts positivity. Your generosity will be reciprocated with solid support that will make the operating environment less threatening for your team. They will be welcomed by others and get the help they need to meet their goals. At times, even exceptions will be made for them.

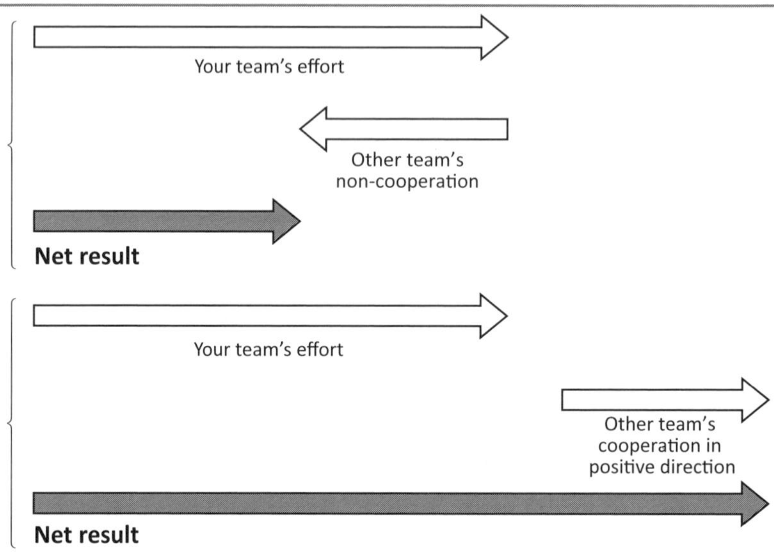

FIGURE 11: **The Multiplier Effect**

Key Takeaways

- Your willingness to appreciate the work of your rivals will set you up as a potential candidate to lead larger teams in the future.
- With you as their ambassador of goodwill, your team's successes will be celebrated by most. So be a magnanimous Credy, and don't let false ego stop you from rooting for others.
- The natural tendency of most teams is to work in silos, because reaching out takes effort. Credy leaders create an environment where their team members are not shy to ask others for support.
- Cheering for your internal competitors will encourage a positive cultural shift within your own team.

Self-Evaluation

Reflect on how intentionally and how often you appreciate those outside your team. Evaluate yourself with the following questions:

- Do you realise that support from internal collaborators is critical to your team's mission?
- Do you consciously look for positive qualities in other people and teams?
- Do you make the effort to commend your rivals' achievements?

Now, give yourself Credy Points based on your behaviour in the above context. Pick the appropriate option:

- ○ Always behave like a Credy: 10 Credy points
- ○ Mostly behave like a Credy: 7 Credy points
- ○ Sometimes behave like a Credy, sometimes like a Goofy: 4 Credy points
- ○ Always behave like a Goofy: 0 Credy points

*'Insaan ka kartavya hota hai koshish karna...
kaamyabi nakaamyabi sab Uske haath mein hai.'*

12/36

Backfired Decision? Just Disown It! A Classic Goofy Escape

*H*AVE YOU EVER *heard a leader say, 'When did I say that?' or 'No, I didn't mean that' or 'You should have asked me!'? There is nothing wrong with these statements, unless they are blatant lies told by a leader when things haven't turned out as expected. They show that the leader has decided to insulate himself from the debacle. They also show that the leader doesn't have an ounce of credibility in him to take ownership of the decisions and actions that led to the failure.*

Sometimes, the decisions we make at work backfire on us. This can happen either because the decision itself was faulty or because it was not accepted by people at large. This non-acceptance can range from mild disagreement to major retaliation. Salvaging such situations is a tough task that exposes a leader's Credy or Goofy behaviour to his peers and subordinates, if not the entire organisation.

At times, even if a decision is well received, the actions that follow are not taken well by stakeholders. While those actions may have been carried out at the leader's direction, it is the team members who face the wrath of the affected parties. I have been at the receiving end of many such brickbats in my career, all because I executed decisions made by my leadership. While my Credy leaders always stood by me like a rock, Goofys just left me to fend for myself.

One such incident happened when my leader, a Credy, asked me to get some information from one of our franchises. It was an uncommon request, but it was well within the terms of our business agreement. I communicated the requirement to the franchise's business head, explaining why we needed the information. But when the franchise owner found out, he called me to say he was quite furious with us, and with me in particular.

When my leader learned about this, he called the franchise owner right away to clarify that the request had come from him. He took full responsibility for the issue, knowing well that it could even lead to a complaint to his superiors.

He could have conveniently asked me to handle the situation on my own or, worse, questioned my approach. But he did none of that. With one phone call, he saved my day-to-day working relationship with the franchise team, which, if ruined, would have severely hampered our business. His support gave me the confidence to execute my duties fearlessly.

Over the next three years with this Credy leader, I achieved results that can only be termed phenomenal. By making tough decisions and standing by them, I changed the way business was carried out with our franchises and dealerships. There were definitely occasions when I faced retaliation or didn't perform as well as expected, but never once did I doubt that my decisions wouldn't get my leader's backing. That made me strong and determined to come back smarter and stronger after every debacle.

Years later, I faced a similar situation with a Goofy leader. We had jointly made a decision regarding annual appraisals, based on which I gave annual ratings to all eighteen members of my team.

As it turned out, one team member was unhappy with his rating. These things happen, but this fellow reacted quite unpleasantly and told me bluntly that he was not at all satisfied with his appraisal. I tried to explain, but he was not pacified. Instead, he decided to bypass the hierarchy and went directly to my Goofy leader. I use the term 'bypass' because he chose not to inform me about the interaction.

This, too, is not unheard of, but what followed was certainly upsetting in many ways. First, my Goofy senior did not bother to take me into confidence before discussing the matter with my team member. Worse, instead of explaining the rationale behind the rating, he completely disowned it and put the entire blame on me. To show his magnanimity, he overturned my decision and upgraded the employee's rating.

The biggest jolt was that I learned all of this not from him but from the HR department.

Obviously, being undermined by my own senior left me red-faced, but there was also another problem. Thanks to his goofiness, we lost an opportunity to give the right feedback to a disgruntled employee. A poor precedent was set forever. After this incident, I lost whatever little respect I had for this Goofy.

Unfortunately, that is how things work in *Goofiland.* While Credy leaders gladly accept responsibility for their decisions and actions, Goofys will go to any length to justify their bad decisions. Mind you, it is not about foolhardy bravery; it is a question of taking ownership and understanding your responsibilities as a leader. Things will not always unfold as you want them to, especially when it comes to people's reactions to your decisions, but it is how you act in these moments that will build or break your credibility.

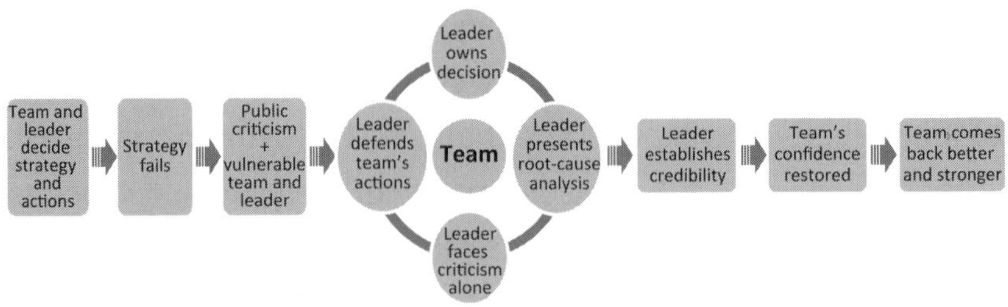

FIGURE 12: **The Shield Effect**

Key Takeaways

- Own them! Yes, own your decisions, as well as those you authorised. If a mistake happens, accept it. Taking ownership of your mistakes doesn't feel as bad as it sounds.
- If a decision backfires, don't try to push it under the rug or pass the blame. People can see what you are doing.
- It's good to be a smart leader, but don't confuse smartness with an attitude of not accepting your mistakes.
- When things go wrong, remind yourself that you have much more to offer as a leader. You will produce many wins in the future, and this one defeat shouldn't affect you so much.

Self-Evaluation

Reflect on your willingness to own your decisions and actions as a leader. Evaluate yourself with the following questions:

- Do you stand by your decisions no matter what the outcome?
- Do you readily admit your mistakes?
- Do you agree that setting the right precedent is the hallmark of credible leadership?

Do you realise that not backing the decisions you authorised can kill your team's motivation to execute them?

Now, give yourself Credy Points based on your behaviour in the above context. Pick the appropriate option:

- ○ Always behave like a Credy: 10 Credy points
- ○ Mostly behave like a Credy: 7 Credy points
- ○ Sometimes behave like a Credy, sometimes like a Goofy: 4 Credy points
- ○ Always behave like a Goofy: 0 Credy points

'Arre bhai kehna kya chahte ho...'

13/36

From Confusion to Clarity: How Credys Cut Through Jargon

IMAGINE BEING IN a foreign country where you don't understand the language, and even your guide, who is supposed to help you communicate with the locals, has limited knowledge of a common tongue. It may not be catastrophic, but it would certainly be frustrating and a waste of time. The same is true for the jargonised and jumbled vocabulary used in organisations – it confuses people, causes misunderstandings, and slows things down.

Jargon is omnipresent in the corporate world. In many organisations, having an internal lingo is even considered a matter of pride. People seem to believe that it gives them some sort of distinction, with some proudly boasting of 'our own world with our own vocabulary'. In my experience, an excess of abbreviations, acronyms, and other mumbo jumbo, which can all be termed as jargon, causes nothing but confusion and chaos.

Most people use jargon out of habit or just to make an impression. Some even love to coin new terms that can be 'patented' in their name. It would be safe to say that many of these terms are born in meetings, from where they spread like wildfire. Without exception, the meaning of the term gets distorted into multiple versions when it reaches others who were not privy to its creation. So, now, the same word has different meanings for different people.

When everyone is left to interpret the message in their own way, efforts are spread in multiple directions, productivity gets diluted, and precious work hours are wasted. But the worst is when a leader, who is supposed to be the de-jargoniser for his team, is in love with jargon. In such cases, the confusion runs deeper and lasts longer.

Once, shortly after joining an organisation considered a global leader in its domain, I received an email from my leader. It read: 'Pls make FOT deck using ABP data points and previous MOM.' I knew that MOM meant minutes of meeting, but FOT deck and ABP data were a mystery to me.

To my amusement, none of my colleagues knew their exact meanings either. There were two or three versions doing the rounds, all of which seemed like very organisation-specific lingo.

After a lot of digging, I found my answers. FOT was short for Franchise Operating Team, and ABP was Annual Business Program. Who would have guessed!

In one Indian company, the abbreviation BRM is used liberally by everyone from the managing director to the security guards. The term has been around for years, yet no one really knows what it means. Some call it Better Review Mechanism, others think it's Business Review Meeting or Board Review Meeting, and yet others are convinced that it means Business Review by Management.

Two of the weirdest terms I've encountered in my career are WTF meetings (short for Weekly Task Force) and GAP (short for the slogan Grow, Achieve, Progress). Yes, absurdly funny!

Let me be clear that I'm not strictly against the use of jargon. Use of process-specific terminology can be helpful in certain contexts. It can speed things up. It is the reckless use of jargon I oppose, as it invariably leads to misunderstandings and delays.

Another kind of jargonisation happens in organisations when communication is sent out to a large group via an email or a text message. Now, this message needs to be clearly understood by all receiving parties. Any gaps in understanding can lead to wrong actions and inaccurate results.

This scenario is typically seen in the aftermath of meetings, when one of the attendees shoots an email to a large number of people, including some who weren't even present at the meeting. Every recipient is now supposed to take some action, but there's a problem: the proceedings and action points read more like cryptic code. This happens when the sender assumes that everyone will understand the message and know what to do just because he does. What follows is complete chaos.

This is where Credy leaders do things differently. They look out for jargon words frequently encountered by their team and explain them in the context they are used. In other words, they actively *de-jargonise* communication for their team by explaining it in the simplest way possible.

Credys also consciously avoid inventing new jargon or popularising existing terms. Their vision and goals are much larger than the foolish habit of creating a jargonised organisation.

I had a Credy leader who explained day-to-day jargon so clearly that there was never any confusion in the team. In fact, shortly after I joined the organisation, he familiarised me with the common lingo spoken there. This helped me a lot. He was also a natural at predicting potential misunderstandings. He reviewed every important communication we sent out and coached us whenever possible on how to make our communication as foolproof as possible to get the desired response from the receiving party.

Thanks to his clear communication and the strong alignment we shared, my time with this leader was a fantastic experience with zero confusion and minimum rework. From him, I learned how to pre-empt situations where my team could get caught up in jargon and what to do if that happened.

In *Goofiland*, things work differently. Goofys love to overuse jargon and leave others to figure things out. This is not always intentional; they simply don't have the empathy to anticipate how difficult it might be for others to decode their words. And if you go to them for clarification, they will never explain what needs to be done. Instead, you will get a standard response like 'Didn't you read my email?' or 'Call that guy (some random person in the organisation) and ask him!'

I had a Goofy leader whose meetings were rife with tired office jargon: 'paradigm shift', 'value proposition', 'drill down', 'circle back', 'CAC', 'LTV', 'SLA', 'ROI', 'ROA', and so on*. Not that these terms are unknown or meaningless, but using them excessively doesn't help. What helps is simple and straightforward communication.

I've also come across another type of *Goofism*: leaders who derive pleasure in knowing things that others don't. But withholding information has it consequences, as my team learned the hard way.

At a meeting of senior leadership to formulate the next fiscal budget, my Goofy leader was the only representative from

**CAC: Customer Acquisition Cost; LTV: Life-Time Value; SLA: Service Level Agreement; ROI: Return on Investment; ROA: Return on Assets.*

our department. After the meeting, the finance team sent out a budget template to all departments requesting their individual requirements. When we asked our leader for guidance, his response was, 'Fill it like you did last year.' That was the only direction from his side.

With no help coming from our leader, one of us consolidated the team's requirements and put them in the template. Our Goofy leader did not even look at the spreadsheet before forwarding it to the finance team.

Shortly afterwards, we received a humiliating rejection from the finance folks. It turned out that they wanted month-wise data, not annual figures. When we asked why their template did not specify this, they said our leader had assured them he would communicate the requirement to us.

They also said that we needed to justify every request exceeding ten thousand dollars. Both requirements had been communicated during the meeting, but our Goofy leader never passed them on. Consequently, the entire worksheet had to be redone, not to mention the embarrassment we faced for holding up the entire budget approval process.

While we were still nursing our wounds, we heard that our Goofy leader commented to someone how incompetent we were as a team.

As a leader, clear communication is one of your key responsibilities. If you dislike confusion and delays, you need to be at your A game when it comes to simplifying things for your team. De-jargonise where possible, and don't expect others to match your knowledge. Instead, meet them where they are and explain accordingly.

By now, you must be feeling like a MORON when it comes to using jargon. Don't get me wrong! MORON here stands for Mindful, Optimistic, Resourceful, Outstanding, and Noble.

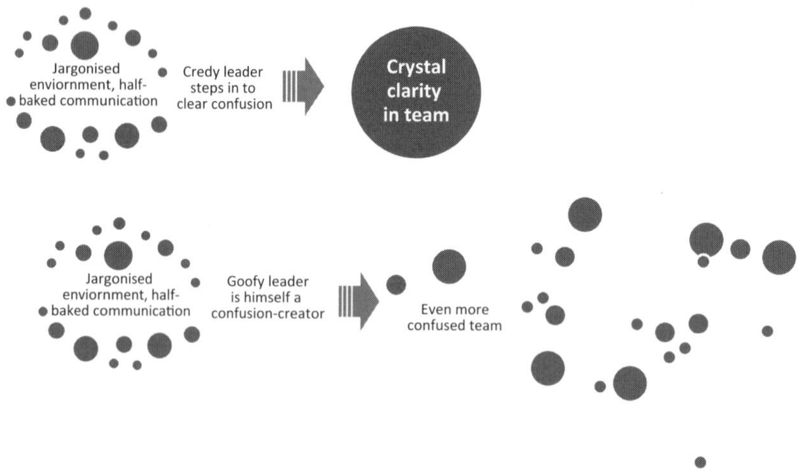

FIGURE 13: **The Reduction-Amplification Dichotomy**

Key Takeaways

- Boisterous jargonisation doesn't just hamper productivity; it leads to misunderstandings and resentment.
- Your team will have great respect for you for being 'simple', which here means making sure they clearly understand the tasks, concepts, data points, meeting summaries, and any other communication relevant to their work.
- When you cannot eliminate jargon, ask yourself whether people will clearly understand your message. If not, simplify it.
- Build a glossary to familiarise new hires and external parties with terms specific to your industry, organisation, and department.

Self-Evaluation

Reflect on how well you handle jargon and communication gaps as a leader. Evaluate yourself with the following questions:

- Do you de-jargonise difficult and confusing terms for your team?
- Are you crystal clear in your communication with your colleagues, vendors, clients, and others?
- Do you often face situations where your team executes a task differently than intended?

Now, give yourself Credy Points based on your behaviour in the above context. Pick the appropriate option:

- ○ Always behave like a Credy: 10 Credy points
- ○ Mostly behave like a Credy: 7 Credy points
- ○ Sometimes behave like a Credy, sometimes like a Goofy: 4 Credy points
- ○ Always behave like a Goofy: 0 Credy points

'Bada aadmi agar banna ho ... to choti harkatein mat karna.'

14/36

Workplace Surveys: Fair or Farcical?

HOW WOULD YOU feel if you asked your leadership for a new printer as your team takes multiple printouts daily and the common printer is already overloaded, but the leadership does nothing about it? Yet the same leadership spends weeks designing and running an annual survey with questions like 'Do you have the right equipment to execute your duties?' This is a classic example of how some senior Goofys operate. The goofiest of all go even further: they simply don't bother to act even on the genuine concerns raised in employee surveys. They have all the power to make positive changes in the organisation, but they always find a way to avoid doing what is necessary. Now, imagine the opposite. How would you feel if your leadership acknowledged your pain points and promptly tried to resolve them instead of waiting for some survey? I bet you would feel awesome.

It is human beings that build and grow organisations, yet their voices are seldom heard in the larger scheme of things. There is a lot of talk about inclusivity, but it's rarely practised. One fancy invention that claims to address employee concerns is the annual satisfaction survey. These surveys are supposed to bridge the gap between expectations and ground realities, but the way they are conducted is often a joke.

I once joined a company where, in my very first interaction with senior leadership, one leader proudly talked about their annual employee satisfaction survey. He said that the organisation had been consistently scoring well in all areas, which, according to him, was proof that people were quite happy. To me, this itself was a red flag. No survey worth its salt gets only positive results across the board.

My apprehensions soon proved right, when I found that many people were dissatisfied with the leadership to the level of being distressed.

Before long, it was time for another annual survey, which turned out to be a big farce. In fact, I was baffled by the sheer goofiness of the process.

To start with, the survey was conducted using a physical form containing ten to twelve questions. This was the first flaw, as people worried their handwriting could be traced back to them and their feedback could be held against them. Second, participants were asked to assemble in a hall where the entire leadership team was already present. This meant that they had to fill out the survey under the scrutinising eyes of their superiors.

The third flaw was even more troubling. After writing their responses, people had to place the form in an envelope and hand it directly to HR, the very folks who had organised the survey. Confidentiality is the fundamental premise of any such survey, but there was absolutely none here. Nor was there any integrity, as some leaders took their entire teams aside to complete the survey in private and then personally submitted the forms to HR. Those people clearly took the survey under duress.

Finally, the questionnaire was only in English, despite common knowledge that over half the employees were not fluent in the language.

I will not go into the questions asked in the survey, as that would require a discussion of its own, but here's one example: 'How many children do you have?' When I asked the HR head how this question was relevant to employee satisfaction, he had no answer. There were many other unnecessary inclusions and some critical exclusions.

All in all, it was tragically comical to see senior management ignore grievances all year and then conduct this mockery of a survey. But even more hilarious were the so-called analysis and action plan that followed. Did we really need an annual survey to find out that the watercooler hadn't been working for over ten months?

This experience aside, I don't believe all surveys are useless. Done properly, they can reveal issues that could go unnoticed otherwise. But what about the team member who proactively comes to you with a problem? His voice is as important as the voices or views captured in an annual ritual.

In my experience, the best leaders listen and act on valid concerns as and when they arise. I've had the privilege of working with one such leader, who encouraged us to voice our issues early so they wouldn't accumulate into bigger problems. Even when he could not offer us a favourable solution, he made sure that we felt heard and understood.

A fine leader who was loyal to his employer but equally concerned for his team, he never acted as a mere messenger of senior management. When he took our concerns to them, he explained the issue in detail and even suggested possible solutions. When conveying the resolution back to us, he backed it up with reason and logic. This approach positioned him as a strong leader among his direct and indirect teams. He earned a loyal following that wasn't driven by hierarchy or compulsion.

It's not having the loudest voice but being a supportive listener that makes you a Credy leader.

Grievances are part of any workplace, but, as we saw above, what people value more than the solution is the intent and approach of their leader. But Goofy leaders, even when they receive first-hand feedback from an aggrieved team member, don't consider it worth acting upon.

Another bitter truth is that annual surveys, which were invented to reveal hidden grievances, are now predominantly used for two reasons: to create the illusion that the management cares about people, and to market the organisation as a great employer.

If you are in a leadership position, resist the temptation to run farcical surveys just to show how much you 'care'. People can easily see through these gimmicks, especially if you took no concrete action after earlier surveys. In any case, if you think an annual survey will give you an honest picture of employee satisfaction, you're doomed at the start itself. People rarely tell the truth in these surveys. Some stay silent for fear of reprimand, while others exaggerate their concerns and unfairly vent out against certain people or processes.

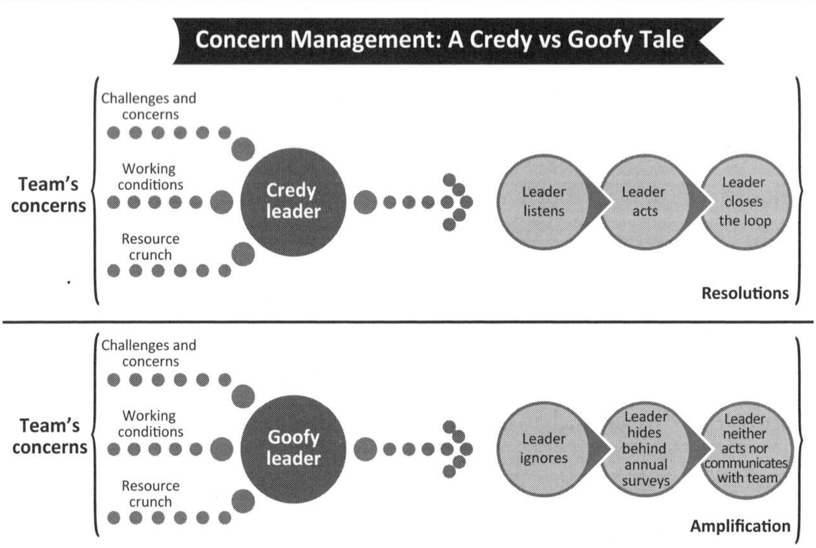

FIGURE 14: **Dissatisfaction Amplified**

Key Takeaways

- Most of the time, you know how your team is feeling, what concerns they have, and which of those concerns are genuine. The Credy approach is to filter out valid issues and address them without delay.
- People are more frustrated when their voices are ignored than when they are heard but not given a favourable resolution. Your goal should be to eliminate the issue: either provide a solution or clearly explain why something cannot be done.
- When you show concern for your team members, most of them will learn to understand the limitations and challenges you face on their behalf.
- Remember, dissatisfaction among your team members is like a festering wound. The more you ignore it, the worse it gets.

Self-Evaluation

Reflect on how much you care about your team's welfare. Evaluate yourself with the following questions:

- Do you take the time to listen to your team members?
- Do you address concerns as they arise or prefer to wait for a feedback survey?
- Do you feel responsible for the well-being of your team?

Now, give yourself Credy Points based on your behaviour in the above context. Pick the appropriate option:

- ○ Always behave like a Credy: 10 Credy points
- ○ Mostly behave like a Credy: 7 Credy points
- ○ Sometimes behave like a Credy, sometimes like a Goofy: 4 Credy points
- ○ Always behave like a Goofy: 0 Credy points

'Bade bade deshon mein
aisi choti-choti baatein hoti rehti hain, Senorita'.

15/36

Failing Boldly: Cultivating Fearlessness from Setbacks

'I TOLD YOU SO!' Have you ever heard these words from your leader after a decision you took went south? I'm guessing you have, many times. These words don't do anything except make people feel guilty in the present and fearful in the future. But they hurt even more when they come from a leader who was taken into confidence at every step. When an outcome isn't favourable, some leaders distance themselves from the decisions that led to it. Of course, there are times when the leader wasn't directly involved in planning or execution because his team had the necessary authority. Still, no plan can ever be just your 'team's plan'. It should always be 'our plan'. A Credy leader goes a step further. When a plan executed by his team doesn't unfold as expected, he takes ownership and turns it into 'his' plan. This empowers the team to make bold decisions and take risks without fear. A Goofy does the opposite. When things go wrong, he announces that he had nothing to do with the plan. This breeds mistrust and frustration and discourages people from taking risks or innovating in the future.

In business, plans are made and decisions are taken with certain outcomes in mind. We use the available facts, the wisdom and experience of our colleagues, and our gut instinct to try and achieve something extraordinary. That said, no plan is ever perfect and no outcome can be accurately predicted. There will be roaring successes, partial wins, non-achievements, and even complete losses.

Whatever the outcome of our efforts, one fundamental rule of good leadership is to never saddle poor results onto your team members. Saying 'I did it!' when things go well and 'You did it!' when they don't is a sign of weak leadership. Scapegoating might help you survive that one review meeting with your bosses, but it will ruin your reputation forever. Moreover, if your team constantly sees you as a buck-passer, they too will learn to make excuses and shirk responsibility.

As discussed earlier in the book, in times of success, credible leaders step aside and let their team lift the trophy. Similarly, when things go wrong, these bold visionaries come forward to take the blame and shield the team.

This reminds me of an experience with a Credy leader years ago. We were facing a significant shortfall in our annual revenue that year. To make up for the deficit, I designed a sales promotion event and pitched it to my leader. While he didn't exactly love the idea, he agreed to give it a try when I insisted.

As luck would have it, the event didn't go as well as I had hoped. You could say it was a 'semi-failure'. I presented the results to my leader expecting a reaction like 'I told you so!', 'You don't listen!', or 'You wasted so much money!'

To my surprise, his response was just the opposite. He made no negative remarks and instead analysed the event in detail. Like any good leader, he started by mentioning the positives, then gave constructive inputs on what could have been done better. He encouraged me to try again.

With his support and guidance, I organised the same event the following month, and the results were far better this time. At the next department meeting, he called it an 'exemplary success story'. He made no mention of the first event, nor claimed credit for the success. Full credit was given to me.

This experience had a big effect on me. From a cautious performer, I transformed into an enthusiastic team member who wasn't afraid to take risks or propose new ideas.

In complete contrast, I worked with a Goofy who discouraged every idea my teammates and I brought to him. When things went wrong, he was quick to shift the blame to us. And when he couldn't find a valid reason to blame us, he would call us incompetent and complain that we never listened to him – never admitting that every decision was made with his approval and he knew of every small development along the way. He even reprimanded us for taking leaves.

This Goofy's strategy was plain and simple: 'In victory, I will take the medal, and in failure, you will take the bullet.' While we learned to live with this, a bigger problem was his complete lack of honesty and his habit of disowning even his own decisions. Basically, he was terrified of being held accountable for failure.

All in all, he was nothing more than a spectator and a devout critic of our work. Instead of leading from the front, he watched from the sidelines, waited for results, and then took a stand based on those results. He conveniently forgot that long before he became our leader, we had been smashing record after record with our performance.

Under his leadership, we felt constantly under threat and lost the zeal to go beyond our assigned duties. 'Our leader is a thankless, gutless, hawkish Goofy, so let's play safe and do the bare minimum.' That became the general outlook in the team.

I have seen many leaders play this game with their teams. Fortunately, I have also worked with gutsy Credys who encouraged me to take risks and stood by my decisions regardless of the outcome. Ultimately, this is what decides how far people will be willing to stretch themselves to help your accomplish your mission.

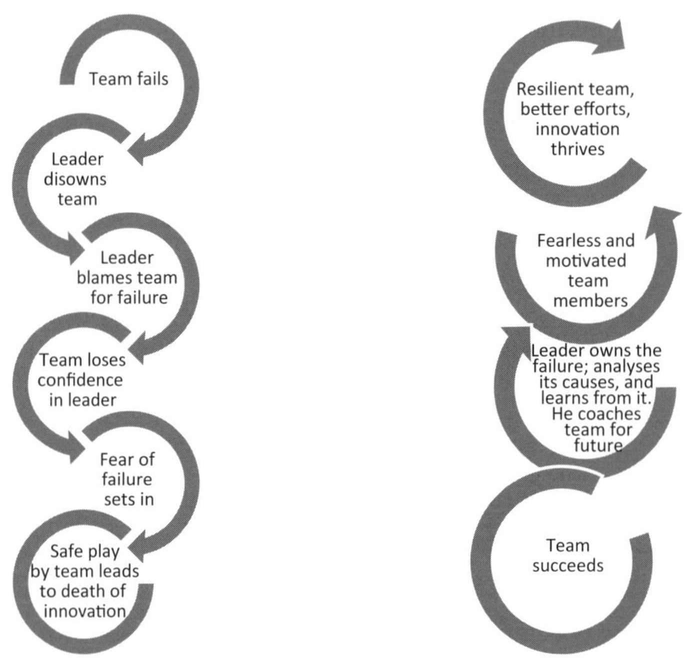

FIGURE 15: **A Vicious Negative Spiral vs A Virtuous Positive Spiral**

Key Takeaways

- Passing the buck to your team might look like a clever move, and you might even wear it like a badge of honour, but don't forget to write GOOFY on it in big and bold letters.

- While success is a shared achievement, it is a leader's privilege to shoulder responsibility for failure. I call it a privilege because only a leader is looked upon to take the blame in tough times. Accept this privilege with grace. It will elevate your stature among your team members and onlookers alike.
- Be ready to face unpleasant reactions when you stand by your team in tough moments. In return, you will be rewarded with a bold group of loyalists who will play not for their personal glory but to make you a winner. I would say it's a good bargain for those fleeting unpleasant moments.
- Lastly, taking the blame doesn't mean that you should bow your head and start apologising. It means to acknowledge failure with confidence and insight, backed by a root-cause analysis, lessons learned, and a plan for course correction.

Self-Evaluation

Reflect on how you react when a decision made by your team ends in failure. Evaluate yourself with the following questions:

- Do you have the sensibility to support well-meaning and well-intentioned team members in times of failure?
- Do you take responsibility for subpar performance even when most of the decision-making and execution was done by your team members?
- Do you have the courage to take the blame for your team's failures?

Now, give yourself Credy Points based on your behaviour in the above context. Pick the appropriate option:

- ○ Always behave like a Credy: 10 Credy points
- ○ Mostly behave like a Credy: 7 Credy points
- ○ Sometimes behave like a Credy, sometimes like a Goofy: 4 Credy points
- ○ Always behave like a Goofy: 0 Credy points

'Ek chutki sindoor ki keemat tum kya jaano Ramesh Babu.'

'Ek Team ki bandwidth ki ahemiyat tum kya jaano Goofy babu.'

16/36

The Goofy Trap of Unrealistic Commitments

Even if a team has all the necessary competencies, there is a limit to what it can accomplish in a given timeframe without sacrificing quality and while still managing a healthy work-life balance. Choosing which battles to fight is a dilemma faced by every leader, and it calls for two skills: the ability to gauge your team's bandwidth and the good sense to decline additional tasks when necessary. Your credibility is directly impacted by your ability to say yes or no to extra workload. While saying yes is easier as it saves the moment, sometimes a firm no is what protects your team from overwhelm and burnout.

Most of us find it hard to say no. We can't help it – it is how we have been programmed since childhood. But this conditioning leads us to spread ourselves too thin in all aspects of life, including work. We see saying no as a sign of weakness, when in fact it can be very empowering.

One of the finest qualities of a leader is to know the collective bandwidth of his team along with the individual capacity of each team member. This helps him make a judgement call when additional work is pushed onto his team by others. I see it as a judgement call because it needs careful consideration of many factors: the team's competence, their current volume of work, how urgent the task is, whether another team is better equipped for the job, the glory attached to taking on a new responsibility, the work satisfaction the team may draw from the work, and so on.

Here, too, I have come across two categories of leaders. The first kind are ambitious but practical when it comes to managing workload. This practical approach comes from the hard work they have done through the years. They know how to calibrate their ambitions to the resources at their disposal. In other words, they know the trade-offs. More importantly, they know that pushing people for more is good, but it is self-sabotaging beyond a point.

The second kind of leaders are also ambitious, but they are theoretical masters. They have never done the work or delivered a quality job. As a result, they lack the experience to assess the time and effort required for a task. Everything looks doable to them, but they are grossly wrong most of the time.

These theoretical masters also have a very weak understanding of the depth of their own resources. Just to project themselves as super-efficient and capable leaders, they give their team members so much to do that they end up doing nothing at all.

Worse, to get you to honour their exaggerated commitments, they will guilt-trip you with random anecdotal references of how a certain person accomplished way more in a similar situation, with no mention of what all was missed in the process. The trouble is, most of these stories are completely fabricated.

The best way to deal with such elements is to let them know in clear terms what you can and cannot do. There will be bruises, but bruises are better than burial!

I had a Goofy leader who habitually made unrealistic commitments on behalf of the team. Forget refusing additional work, he never even tried to calibrate the right timelines by which we could deliver the job. His understanding of the task-resource equation was woeful, as was his ability to differentiate must-do, good-to-do, and junk tasks.

His obsession with overcommitment – and the resulting nonfulfilment on our part – did permanent damage to our team. People lost faith in our ability to fulfil even our core deliverables.

Goofys get lured by the pleasure of raising their hand for additional work without checking if they have the necessary resources. No wonder their teams are perpetually overworked, always under pressure to meet deadlines, and making corrections as they go along. In the end, despite all this effort, they feel little sense of achievement.

Taking up new challenges is easy; what's difficult is delivering them right. As I see it, however big or small the stage, no show is any day better than a poor show.

Credys work in a completely opposite way. They do believe in stretching their resources, but not to the point of breaking them. They prefer assigning fewer tasks to their team members rather than forcing them to juggle multiple tasks and then scramble to deliver even the basics. In other words, Credys like to take a bite that's the right size for their mouth.

I had a Credy leader like that. His credibility in the team was so high that we never objected to any extra work he brought to us. We trusted his ability to weigh the pros and cons before making a commitment on our behalf. His reputation outside the team was equally credible. If he agreed to a project or assignment, people knew it would be done well in every respect. If he turned down a request, he gave a valid reason for it.

Think of it this way: a team is like a ship and team members are the crew. Tasks are passengers who come onboard this ship. As the captain of the ship, you cannot accept an infinite number of passengers. Every addition beyond the ship's capacity puts pressure on the crew and increases the risk of capsizing. At some point, you will have to say a firm no to additional passengers to keep the ship from sinking.

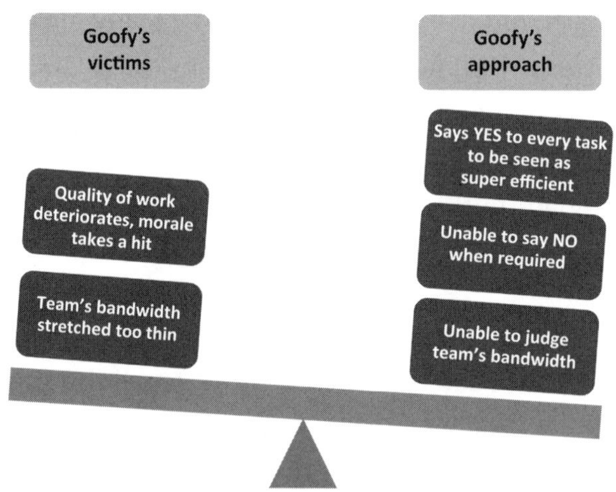

FIGURE 16: **The Goofy Misbalance**

Key Takeaways

- It took me many years to learn that you can say no and still be a good team player. This may sound contradictory, but think again!
- If you cannot judge your team's capacity, you are a Goofy. But if you know their capacity and still choose to overburden them, you are an even bigger Goofy!
- Committing to what you cannot deliver makes you look bad as a leader. In the end, neither your team nor those who trusted you with the task will respect you.

- Learn to choose your battles. It may give you a moment of pride to agree to an unrealistic goal or task, but after that it's a downhill slope of stress and frustration.
- When you need to say no, say it loud and clear. You may upset some people, but it's better than having to cut a sorry figure later.

Self-Evaluation

Reflect on how conscious you are of your team's bandwidth and how gutsy you are when it comes to rejecting excess work. Evaluate yourself with the following questions:

- Do you understand that completing every task requires adequate resources in terms of people, money, material, and time?
- Do you consult your team before committing to additional work on their behalf?
- Can you say no to your superiors and justify it as well?

Now, give yourself Credy Points based on your behaviour in the above context. Pick the appropriate option:

- ○ Always behave like a Credy: 10 Credy points
- ○ Mostly behave like a Credy: 7 Credy points
- ○ Sometimes behave like a Credy, sometimes like a Goofy: 4 Credy points
- ○ Always behave like a Goofy: 0 Credy points

'Sara sheher mujhe Lion ke naam se janta hai.'

17/36

Image Matters!

A LEADER'S IMAGE is the ultimate power play. It's a weapon that can be used to command respect or crush one's credibility. Invariably, leaders with a strong executive presence, no-nonsense approach, and cordial disposition are taken more seriously than leaders who come across as egoistic, casual, or quarrelsome. To put it simply, when it comes to making an impression, image matters. Moreover, your image as a leader directly affects the image of your team. The stronger your own image, the easier it becomes for your team to maintain a foothold in the ecosystem.

In the professional world, your glory or notoriety steps in long before you do. People view your words, actions, and motives through the lens of the image they have of you. Therefore, a strong and positive image is critical to your success as a leader. But this image should never be fake or manipulated. It should be a true projection of who you are as a person and a leader. Creating a superhero kind of image is counterproductive at best, as it creates false expectations you will not be able to fulfil.

Also, to be of any use, your personal and professional image should be recognised and acknowledged by the key players in your operating environment. By key players, I mean people and departments whose cooperation is critical for your team to work effectively and efficiently. By building a powerful persona, you can get collaboration even from colleagues who are loosely connected to you and are not obliged to support your work.

Let me explain this with a hypothetical scenario. Imagine you are the head of sales at a manufacturing company, and your team regularly organises customer visits to your factory. You may not realise it, but auxiliary departments like hospitality and security have an important role in the success of these visits. It might sound far-fetched, but it's true. The performance of these departments can make or break your customer's experience and, in turn, your efforts to satisfy them.

This is where your image as a leader comes into play. A strong image will get you cooperation from across the board. Your guests will be treated with utmost care and attention. For example, the security team may prioritise gate passes and the hospitality-in-charge may personally attend to your guests. The point to be noted is this: you are not present at these visits, nor do you work closely with these departments, but your image has travelled ahead of you and worked in your favour.

For practical purposes, a strong image means that your subject knowledge, experience, and contributions to the business are well recognised by your peers, juniors, and seniors. It also means you have great interpersonal relationships across departments. This image is built over time, and it is shaped not only by what you say but also by what you don't say, that is, nonverbal communication like your body language, facial expressions, tone of voice, and so on. Social interactions with your colleagues also play a part.

A great leader I worked with in the early days of my career actively worked on cultivating a strong personal image. I can still recall how he conducted himself in meetings and other forums – always charged up and generously supportive of others while firmly standing his ground.

This Credy commanded respect from people across levels, roles, and age groups. His ability to choose when and where to speak and his calm demeanour placed him a notch above the rest. His strong and positive image made our job a lot easier. We were seen as a team that meant business and got attention where it was due.

When it came to resolving our concerns, he believed in direct and open communication. He had no inhibitions to go and speak with anyone in the hierarchy if it helped his team (a rarity among leaders!). But we also knew that he was not going to rescue us from every minor roadblock. He was selective and prudent in his interventions.

In a parallel world, a Goofy leader simply clings to the designation bestowed upon him. His authority and span of influence are limited to his title. He makes his presence felt not by doing any real work but by dominating his subordinates, who are bound by hierarchy to do his bidding.

Such Goofys are boisterous among juniors, silent among peers, and timid among seniors. To make up for their weak image, they resort to brown-nosing their influential colleagues. But this only adds to their image of a paper tiger with a puffed-up ego who lacks what it takes to be a leader.

A leader's image can either amplify his team's work or cast a dark shadow over it. I had a Goofy leader whose poor image created endless hurdles for us. Most of the time, we were either justifying his weak decisions or apologising for his irrational behaviour. It was a constant struggle to distance ourselves from his reputation. No one in the organisation took us seriously.

For a leader, an image once created is difficult to change, so your first impression itself should be appropriate. Besides qualities like punctuality, courteousness, and humility, how you dress, walk, talk, laugh, eat, or even say thank-you or sorry – all of it contributes to your image.

Similarly, every interaction, be it a phone conversation, an email, a meeting, a formal discussion, casual chit-chat, dining with colleagues or clients, attending an event, or even restroom talk, shapes your persona as a leader. Credys are aware of this and adapt themselves to project the image of well-respected and competent leaders.

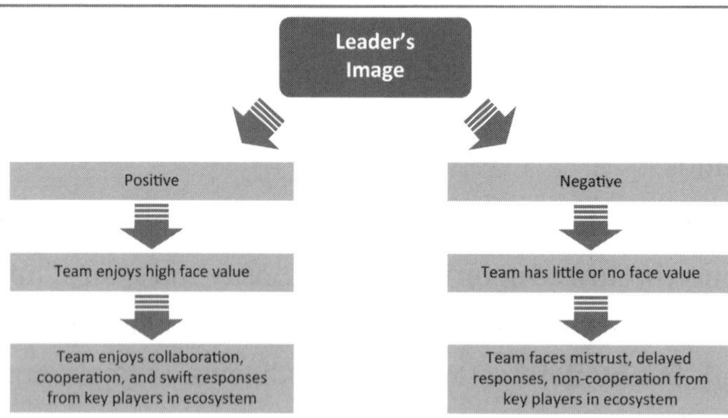

FIGURE 18: **Causes-and-Effect Relationship between a Leader's Image and His Team's Foothold in the Organisation**

Key Takeaways

- Whether or not you accept it, image matters. Your work will ultimately get its due, but it is your everyday conduct that decides how you are perceived by clients, colleagues, and subordinates.
- In a collaborative environment, a lot gets done based on who is asking for it. As their leader, you owe it to your team to exude a strong and confident persona. Your team is seen as a reflection of you, and your image casts a big halo around them.

- Everything you say or do as a leader – your ideas, suggestions, proposals, appreciation, and even displeasure – is first filtered through the lens of *who* said or did it rather than *what* was said or done. This *who* is nothing but your image. Build a positive image so that your words and actions pass through this first filter with ease. This will greatly help your team.

Self-Evaluation

Reflect on whether you know the importance of maintaining a strong personal brand as a leader. Evaluate yourself with the following questions:

- Are you aware that your personal image reflects on your team's competence?
- Do you actively work to build the right image as a professional?
- Do you think people outside your immediate team see you as someone they want to work with or learn from?

Now, give yourself Credy Points based on your behaviour in the above context. Pick the appropriate option:

- ○ Always behave like a Credy: 10 Credy points
- ○ Mostly behave like a Credy: 7 Credy points
- ○ Sometimes behave like a Credy, sometimes like a Goofy: 4 Credy points
- ○ Always behave like a Goofy: 0 Credy points

*'Ye dhai kilo ka haath jab kisi pe padta hai na,
to aadmi uthta nahi, uth jata hai.'*

18/36

Hostility-Free Zone: Creating a Safe Space for Your Team

IN EVERY PROFESSION, you will find people with different motives and egos. For various reasons, some will behave in an uncooperative, unprofessional, or even insulting manner. While we've all faced such colleagues, the chances of a rendezvous with rejection, ridicule, or humiliation are higher when you're seeking cooperation from people outside your core team. As a leader, you should know that before anything else, your team members want to be treated with respect. Just as you expect them to carry out your instructions with enthusiasm and fearlessness, you must be prepared to shield them from insults and attacks by outsiders.

Hostile treatment from colleagues leads to low morale, low confidence, and a fear to carry out one's duties. The more junior people are in their rank, the more vulnerable they are to such attacks. While Credys never overlook these issues, Goofys don't even acknowledge them. The reasons for their indifference can be many: no sense of responsibility, an uncaring attitude towards the team, or fear of being insulted if they confront the wrongdoer.

Whatever the reason, the impact of a Goofy's inaction is always the same: he loses credibility.

Let me share two such incidents that evoked contrasting reactions from my leaders, leading to diagrammatically different outcomes.

In the automobile industry, vehicles are sold through dealer-partners, who are required to follow certain processes and compliances set by the organisation. I was part of a team whose job was to ensure that our dealer-partners adhered to those terms and conditions.

For many months, we had been facing a typical problem: on some pretext or other, some dealers were not refunding the excess money deposited by customers. This was causing dissatisfaction among our customers, not to mention that it was strictly against the company's code of conduct. We had to find a way to stop this malpractice.

Our leader, a seasoned Credy, gave us the go-ahead to come up with a new refund process for the excess payments received from customers. We expected some retaliation from the erring dealers, as their earnings were going to be affected by this move, but our leader assured us of his full support and asked us to proceed without fear.

As expected, there was some backlash when we rolled out the policy, but one particular incident truly demonstrated our leader's ability and willingness to defend us from unjustified attacks.

One of my colleagues visited a key dealership to implement the new refund system. The general manager there was known to have an ego problem. As my colleague explained the new process, the manager kept finding faults in the process and raising baseless objections. My colleague tried to clarify, but this fellow refused to cooperate. He walked out of the meeting and instructed his team to do the same, leaving my colleague alone in the room.

This was extremely humiliating for my colleague. He called our leader, who asked him to leave the dealer's office immediately. We all waited anxiously to see what action our leader would take against this toxic manager, who was drunk on the power he wielded with the blessings of his boss the almighty, the owner of the dealership.

Later in the day, something unprecedented happened. Our leader sent an email to all our dealer-partners, including the dealer in question, with the subject line 'Persona non grata'. He described the events of the day and declared that, going forward, no one from his team was going to interact with the manager who had misbehaved with our colleague. 'It's not about following the process or questioning it. It's about respect,' he wrote. 'Those who don't respect my team will not be tolerated.'

This is how our Credy leader stood up for us and restored my colleague's confidence and pride. He sent out a strong message that nonsensical behaviour by anyone was unacceptable. Shortly afterwards, the general manager in question, who was infamous for undermining authority and demeaning people, was let go by his employer.

A similar incident of poisonous behaviour happened when I was in a different organisation. A colleague of mine visited a dealership for a routine interaction with their sales team. The dealership owner was also present at the meeting. About twenty minutes into the discussion, he abruptly asked my colleague to end the meeting and leave. According to him, my colleague was wasting his staff's time.

Without debating the usefulness of the meeting, let me say that for a young professional in his mid-twenties, this was humiliation of the highest order. My colleague returned to the office and shared the incident with our leader. The least we expected was for our Goofy leader to call up the dealer and express his disapproval. Instead, he laughed as if something funny had happened. He then simply told my colleague not to visit the dealership for a few days and wait for things to get back to 'normal'. This left us all in shock. We felt dejected and betrayed. In one word, we were *Goofified*!

Not surprisingly, the entire team decided to play super-safe from then on. If our Goofy leader didn't even have the courage to counter an unnecessary and unprovoked attack, he could not be trusted to support us in situations that might need an even gutsier response.

These two stories make one thing clear: leadership is not just about giving directions; it's about standing up for those who follow your lead. If you truly want to empower your team, you need to stand up for them, especially when they're made to feel powerless by others.

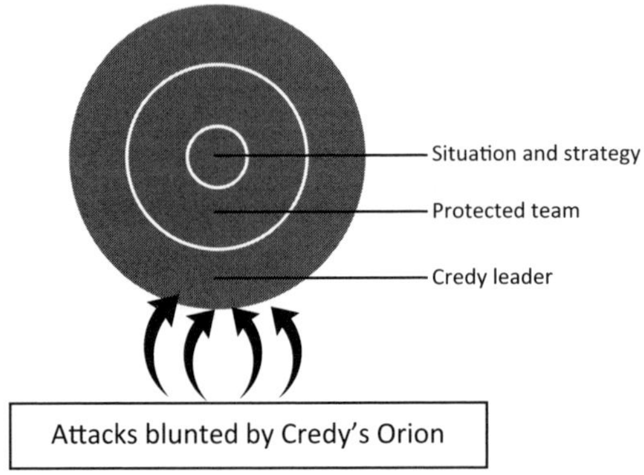

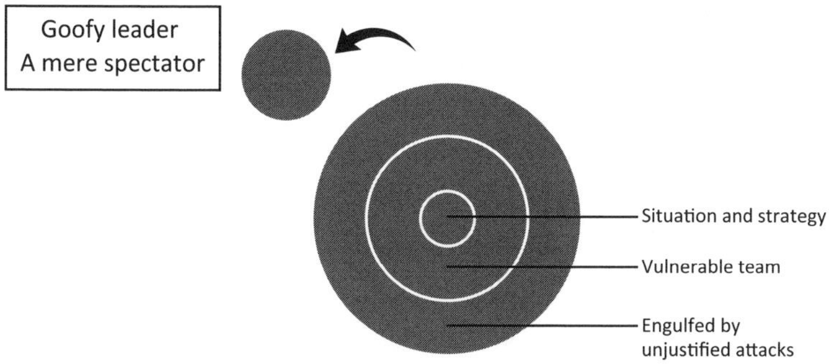

FIGURE 18: **Credy as Protector vs Goofy as Spectator**

Key Takeaways

- Go out of your way to protect your team. I am not asking you to cover up their mistakes or overlook integrity issues, but to stand up for them when they are attacked by people with half-baked knowledge, malicious intentions, or just a habit of attacking others.
- Malicious people cannot be eliminated from any environment, but they can be tackled and countered. In most cases, your team members can handle these characters on their own, but sometimes it may be beyond their capacity or authority to fight back. This is when you need to step in. If you stand up for your team, they will also fight for your cause and vision.

Self-Evaluation

Reflect on how well you protect your team from unjustified attacks while they carry out your vision, direction, and strategy. Evaluate yourself with the following questions:

- Do you always stand up for your team?
- Do you agree that your team members' respect and morale are as important as your own?

Do you have the courage to make decisions that may temporarily affect your business goals but will protect your team from unwarranted hostility?

Now, give yourself Credy Points based on your behaviour in the above context. Pick the appropriate option:

- ○ Always behave like a Credy: 10 Credy points
- ○ Mostly behave like a Credy: 7 Credy points
- ○ Sometimes behave like a Credy, sometimes like a Goofy: 4 Credy points
- ○ Always behave like a Goofy: 0 Credy points

Inspirer

'Jali ko aag kehte hain,
bujhi ko raakh kehte hain
jis raakh se barood bane usey Vishwanath kehte hain.'

19/36

Turning Trouble into Triumph: The Power of Credys

BAD TIMES CAN be good, problems can be profitable, and crises can be turned into opportunities – that's how great minds think and act. When everyone else is ready to concede defeat, they calmly dissect the problem to look for an opportunity in the middle of it. Then, they do something unusual, something unprecedented, something big. Where others might crumble under pressure, these real-life heroes use their wisdom to decide whether to go with the flow or to give the situation a positive twist. At a minimum, these positive twists help minimise the losses; at their best, they turn what looks like a catastrophe into a real opportunity.

Life in the corporate world is never dull. Crisis, chaos, ambiguity – all are part of the game. One of the key jobs of a leader is to manage crises as they arise, but Credys and Goofys have very different approaches to crisis management. While Credys try to find opportunity in crisis, Goofys look for a scapegoat to blame.

Moreover, since Goofys hate to leave their comfort zone, they switch to denial mode the moment there's a problem. They avoid facing the issue, avoid being part of the solution, and refuse to learn anything from the experience. This is why you will never see a Goofy willingly take on a challenge.

Credible leaders take the opposite route. Avoiding the problem doesn't even figure in their thought process. Instead, they bravely accept the situation and get down to finding a solution. If an ideal resolution is not possible, they try to make the most of what they have. In other words, they master the art of turning adversity into opportunity. This approach benefits everyone. The team develops a troubleshooting mindset and the organisation becomes more efficient and profitable.

Let me share an example. In the automobile industry, vehicles are sold through a dealer network, which means the strength of your dealer network has a direct impact on your business. More dealers means more business – that is the thumb rule. While working with a leading car manufacturer, I was managing a town in central India. At the time we had three dealers in the area, while our closest rival had two dealers. Things were going well for us, until one of our dealers went defunct. Coincidentally, our competitor recruited a new dealer around the same time. So, from a dealer ratio of 3:2, we suddenly went to 2:3.

This was a serious issue for us, given that we had 50 per cent of the market share while our rival had just 20 per cent. In this industry, it can take up to two years to set up a new dealership, which meant that we could lose valuable market share and get pushed back by years. That would have led to unrecoverable losses. Let me share how my Credy leader handled the situation.

At an industry event, my leader happened to meet the new dealer who had signed up with our rival. A conversation followed, and the dealer revealed that his original plan was to partner with us, but somehow that did not materialise. My leader sensed an opportunity here. What started as a casual conversation turned into a five-hour discussion, by the end of which the dealer had a complete change of heart. He decided to part ways with our rival brand and join us instead.

This was unprecedented, unheard of, and unthinkable in that era. My Credy leader, through his exceptional business acumen and emotional intelligence, had managed to convince this dealer that he was missing out on an opportunity of a lifetime.

Naturally, there were questions about the ethics and norms around poaching a competitor's dealer. To justify his actions, my leader had to do a lot of introspection and a lot of explaining to his seniors. It was a big and bold step for both sides, so the entire upward chain of command was taken into confidence and an organisation-wide signoff was obtained to proceed with the move.

Car dealerships are built around certain organisational norms, and converting a dealership set to our rival's standards was a big challenge. Nevertheless, our entire team rallied behind our leader to ensure everything went well, fully leveraging the foundation he had laid. The dealer was onboarded in precisely seventeen days, a process that normally took two or more years.

The ripple effect of this move was that our defunct dealer had a wake-up call – or should I say a 'perform or perish' call – and started delivering results. The outcome? In a matter of weeks, the 2:3 dealer ratio changed to 4:2. We had thwarted the competition's plans by at least two years, and our market share climbed to 60 per cent. No laws were broken, no unethical actions were taken – it was just a simple but bold business decision in the middle of a crisis that turned things around.

In a free market, it is not only our product or service but also our mindset that competes with our rivals. It takes a winning mindset to even come up with an unorthodox solution, let alone make it happen with breakneck speed. But this is how Credys think and execute. They don't get bogged down by history – they create history.

Goofys, on the other hand, have neither the aptitude nor the inclination to turn a crisis in their favour. When faced with a problem, they resort to conventional defences at best, while the goofier ones simply flee the situation leaving others to clean up the mess. This explains why organisations run by Credys always prevail over those run by Goofys.

FIGURE 19: **Effects of a Leader's Conduct in Crisis**

Key Takeaways

- In a crisis, it's your temperament that is tested more than anything. Whatever the situation, keep your calm.
- Any good leader will try to minimise the impact of a crisis, but Credys, with the proverbial cool hat on their heads, will also have the presence of mind to look for a potential opportunity in the situation.
- By having a wide-angle view of the problem, including the hidden aspects, you can emerge as a Credy leader in the trickiest of situations.

Of course, you need to be at your defensive best when dealing with a problem, but sometimes, when everyone else is running for safety, taking an offensive approach can be the best strategy. What you need is a cool head, belief in yourself, and the confidence to turn things around.

Self-Evaluation

Reflect on how you handle crises as a leader. Evaluate yourself with the following questions:

- Do you face setbacks head-on?
- What is your main concern in a crisis: to find a solution or to look for a scapegoat?
- Are you able to think clearly and do more than just damage control in the middle of chaos?

Now, give yourself Credy Points based on your behaviour in the above context. Pick the appropriate option:

- ○ Always behave like a Credy: 10 Credy points
- ○ Mostly behave like a Credy: 7 Credy points
- ○ Sometimes behave like a Credy, sometimes like a Goofy: 4 Credy points
- ○ Always behave like a Goofy: 0 Credy points

'Wo do the aur tum teen,
phir bhi wapas aagaye khaali haath.
Kya samajh kar aaye the?
Sardar bahot khus hoga?
Sabasi dega?'

Whatever Gabbar Singh was but
he was not a coward Goofy leader.

20/36

Tough Conversations to Address Unprofessional Behaviour and Underperformance

In friendship, we look for total honesty, especially when we may be doing something wrong. Our true friends are the first to point out our mistakes and help us improve. Similarly, to improve our health or our skills, we want guidance from an expert like a doctor or a coach. No one benefits from hearing only kind words and compliments. When we're shown the mirror by a sincere well-wisher, we try to perform better. This is also true for leaders and their teams. Credible leaders know the importance of addressing mistakes and underperformance at the right time and in the right manner. Confronting these issues is never easy, but that's what great leadership is all about.

Regardless of the type or purpose of your work, results will always matter. Poor results call for strong corrective action, particularly when they stem from unprofessional behaviour. The situation calls into question a leader's ability to spot and correct misconduct or negligence in the concerned team member.

Before we proceed, let me explain the connection between bad behaviour and poor results. In the workplace, bad behaviour typically means neglecting to do the right thing – for example, not planning well, not focusing on the quality of execution, communicating poorly, lacking proactiveness, procrastinating, being lethargic, having unnecessary arguments with colleagues, bullying others, and being indifferent to results, to name a few. Note that competence is not the issue here, just bad behaviour. Even when it's not intentional, if left unaddressed, such behaviour can have a snowball effect on the entire team.

While Credy leaders don't hesitate to confront such issues, Goofys close their eyes to the situation. This could be for two reasons: they have the same behavioural issues themselves or they are too timid to have a confrontation.

One of my Credy leaders was exceptional at balancing professional goals and personal rapport. He was friendly and approachable, and we enjoyed his company both at work and afterwards. Even our families met occasionally. But this never stopped him from pointing out a behavioural or performance issue in the team. He never allowed the personal bonhomie to come in the way of hard discussions. When it came to behaviour, in particular, there was zero tolerance.

Like a great coach, he handled issues according to their severity. People were never placed under fire for a minor issue, nor were they let go with a light reprimand for throwing a tantrum.

We admired him for his brutal but genuine feedback – a bitter pill that was served to us sometimes in private and sometimes in front of the whole team. But the hurt was momentary as we knew his intentions were pure. Moreover, he always supported his observations with facts and evidence.

Let me share an example. One of my teammates had a habit of inviting our vendors and dealer-partners for meetings and then making them wait unnecessarily. This wasted everyone's time, but more than that, it was disrespectful to the visitors. Over time, others in the team started showing the same unprofessionalism. As soon as this came to our leader's notice, he called a team huddle and made it clear that such behaviour was unacceptable. We were instructed to be punctual and mindful of others' time or hand over our meetings to someone else.

In his view, the fact that we gave business to our dealers and vendors did not give us licence to treat them poorly. He said that one team member's behaviour reflected on all of us, and it had to stop. The impact of this reprimand was immediate and positive. Our colleague realised his mistake and corrected his behaviour, while others who were mildly 'infected' got the 'treatment' they needed. The best part was that none of us had any hard feelings for our leader, only more admiration.

In the five years I spent with this Credy, I learned two important lessons. First, no matter how soft-hearted or friendly you are as a leader, you should be able to provide constructive criticism to your team members. Second, while people may feel hurt when confronted, deep down, they admire a leader who points out their weak areas and helps them improve.

In contrast, I had a Goofy leader who was a champion of timidity. He never confronted anyone, even when they made a blunder, behaved poorly, stalled the team's progress, or delivered the worst results. He could never call a spade a spade, because he was a people-pleaser who did not want to offend anyone. Or maybe he tolerated slip-ups because he was a master of slip-ups himself.

Let me give you an example of his goofiness. One of my teammates was responsible for preparing the monthly incentive plan for our sales force in the region. It was critical for this plan to be rolled out at the start of the month, preferably on the first day itself. But this fellow would take his own sweet time for no apparent reason other than procrastination or laziness. He would send the document only around the 7th or the 10th, by which point we would lose critical time to motivate our sales teams.

Our Goofy leader was fully aware of the issue. Many of us had requested him to either correct this guy or give the responsibility to someone else. But he did nothing. The problem continued forever and everyone suffered because of his spineless leadership. Contrary to his perception of himself as a popular leader, to us he was nothing more than a toothless tiger.

Leaders who don't call out mistakes or misdemeanour may look easy-going in the present, but in the long run, they are like those bad teachers from school who never taught you anything in class, never gave you difficult tests, and were more than lenient when giving you marks, making you believe that you were doing well. But when faced with the real tests of life, you had a very tough time. No one remembers those teachers fondly.

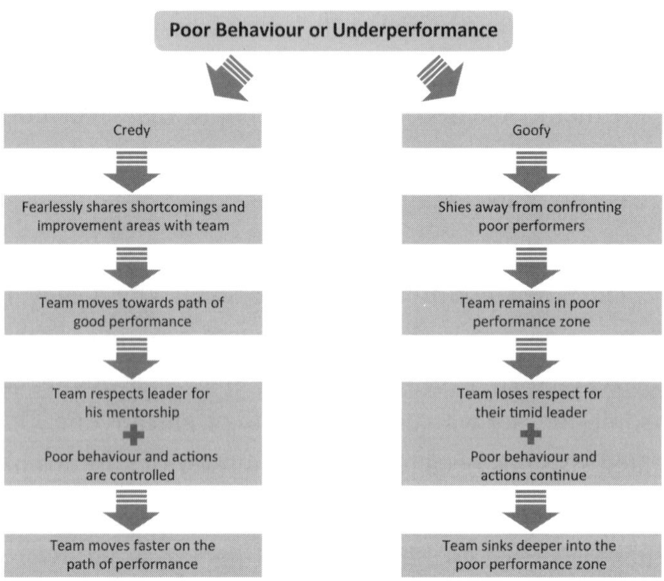

FIGURE 20: **Contrasting Treatment – Contrasting Outcomes**

Key Takeaways

- Leaders, go out and tell your team members in no uncertain terms where and how they could have done better. Have the stomach to give critical feedback even to your most favourite employee. It's your responsibility to point out areas of improvement that could be affecting individual or team performance.

- You need to build a strong team, and for that, you need to eliminate everything from minor issues to fatal flaws. It may give you discomfort, anxiety, and pain, but it has to be done in the interest of the erring team member, those who work with him, and your own self. Plus, discussing the problem gives you a chance to know their side of the story.
- Clinging to a 'good guy' image will only make you a Goofy. Ultimately, people will remember you not for ignoring their faults but for giving them timely feedback that helps them become better human beings and better professionals.

Self-Evaluation

Reflect on how comfortable you are giving constructive feedback to your team members. Evaluate yourself with the following questions:

- Can you spot problematic behaviour in a team member and control it before it spreads to others?
- Do you hesitate to confront your team members even when you know they made a mistake?
- Do you make it a point to not only correct wrong behaviour but also explain your reasoning so that the message gets immediate and permanent acceptance?
- Do you think it's important to build the right culture within your team?

Now, give yourself Credy Points based on your behaviour in the above context. Pick the appropriate option:

- ○ Always behave like a Credy: 10 Credy points
- ○ Mostly behave like a Credy: 7 Credy points
- ○ Sometimes behave like a Credy, sometimes like a Goofy: 4 Credy points
- ○ Always behave like a Goofy: 0 Credy points

'How's the josh?'

21/36

The Art of Recharging Morale After a Setback

IMAGINE YOU'VE TAKEN an exam, played a sports match, or chased any other goal, but despite a wholehearted attempt, you have failed. In such moments, what kind of words would you want to hear from your teacher or coach? What you would like to hear is exactly what team members want to hear from their leader when they have not met expectations. While the debacle needs to be analysed and a better strategy chalked out, first and foremost, people need to regain their lost confidence and morale. And this depends a lot on how their leader acts in the face of failure.

Boosting morale is a fundamental responsibility of any leader. The best leaders know that their reaction to failure can make or break their team's morale, which needs to be brought back quickly to prepare for the next mission. So they ensure that the team recovers fast and moves on.

With Goofys, the low-morale phase is painfully long. This is either because they lack the tact to choose the right words and body language to uplift their team, or because they don't see it as their responsibility to help the team bounce back. As a result, the team languishes in the pit of dejection, which then affects their future performance. This is how Goofys create a loop of failure and low morale.

I had a Credy leader who had an uncanny ability to sense when our motivation was running low. We were a formidable team, but there were times when we fell short of our targets. But never once did he suggest that we were not good enough. On the contrary, his behaviour, gestures, words, and actions constantly reassured us that highs and lows were both part of the business. He repeatedly reminded us that there was no need to beat ourselves up over an occasional setback.

From simple gestures like always carrying a smile, breaking into impromptu pep talk, and organising team lunches to more complex ones like carefully analysing our performance, every action of this leader was mindful and uplifting. Even his pep talks were never surface-level. He would dive deep into the problem areas and somehow always manage to find a silver lining. Only after this groundwork would he do the talking.

After sharing his observations, he encouraged us to brainstorm how we could come back bigger and better. Together, we would come up with strategies to recover the shortfall in our targets. We confidently navigated many rough waters under this Credy's leadership.

Looking back, I realise how masterfully he brought us back into the game, like a symphony master guiding musicians who go out of tune for a moment. He also had the knack to find humour in setbacks. Once, when we missed our quarterly target and were under immense pressure to face the management, he said to us, '*Jab cooker me ho baithe to pressure se kya darna!*' ('Why fear the pressure when you are inside the pressure cooker!')

Of course, any good leader will say nice things and appreciate his team's efforts when results fall short, but if the pep talk is punctuated with a solid cause-and-effect analysis, it sounds more authentic. This is why our leader's words always worked. We trusted his insights, realised our individual mistakes, and converted them into smart learnings.

This in no way means that Credys accept underperformance or non-achievement. They are smart enough to tell genuine effort from complacency and know that each has to be dealt with differently.

Let me summarise what I learned from this Credy leader about restoring morale. There are three important considerations when you are trying to help your team bounce back from failure:

- First, you should not be seen as a leader who is okay with failure all the time. Your behaviour and actions should never convey that success has no value.
- Second, the lessons learned from the defeat must be baked back into the team's work to avoid repeating the same mistakes.
- Lastly, team members who made avoidable mistakes should be given constructive feedback.

In comparison, Goofys fail at their basic duty when the team is feeling dejected. There are three reasons for this goofiness. First, since Goofys don't want to own below-par results, instead of analysing the root cause, they get into fault-finding mode. They are so preoccupied with defending themselves that they fail to see any bright spots in the situation. Second, they fail to understand that their team members are humans, not machines, who need help with mending their shattered morale. Poor results impact everyone and not just the leader. The injury may not be visible but it plays on people's minds. It needs cleaning, bandaging, and proper healing. Third, they lack the intelligence and charisma of Credy leaders, who use their influence and aura to uplift their team members in times of failure.

I had a Goofy colleague who, whenever his team underperformed, made it a point to tell everyone how he had wanted them to work differently but they took his 'golden' advice casually. His goofiness didn't end there. Instead of helping the team recover and move on, he would act in bizarre ways, giving them silent treatment and losing his temper on things as trivial as a mobile phone ringing for a few extra seconds. His body language would swing between lethargy and aggression. All in all, he looked like someone who had lost all control and was living in fear and anger.

His *Goofaniyat* obviously rubbed off on his team. With a broken mindset, they struggled to perform and were trapped in a vicious cycle of defeat after defeat.

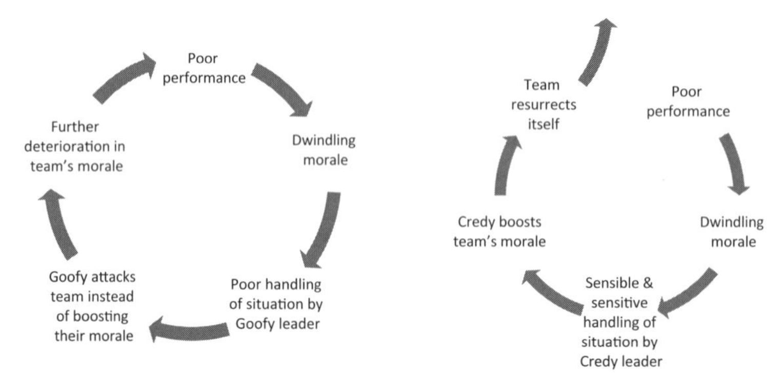

FIGURE 21: **A Team's Confinement in vs Escape from the Vicious Cycle of Failure and Low Morale**

Key Takeaways

- If you want an army of go-getters and risk-takers who know how to bounce back from failure, you need to care about their mental and emotional well-being. Even the best of talents will not perform if their morale is running low.
- Whatever you may think or preach about self-motivation, it doesn't diminish your role as the ultimate motivator for your team. They need reassurance from you that they have the capacity to bounce back. They want to hear from you that you still have confidence in their abilities.
- As a Credy leader, you should know how to tread the fine line between keeping your team motivated and avoiding a culture of complacency.

Self-Evaluation

Reflect on how good you are at re-energising your team in the face of individual or collective failure. Evaluate yourself with the following questions:

- Do you make a conscious effort to bring back the lost morale of your team?
- Do you tend to pass the buck to your team members?
- Are you generally able to see the silver lining around poor performance?

Now, give yourself Credy Points based on your behaviour in the above context. Pick the appropriate option:

- ○ Always behave like a Credy: 10 Credy points
- ○ Mostly behave like a Credy: 7 Credy points
- ○ Sometimes behave like a Credy, sometimes like a Goofy: 4 Credy points
- ○ Always behave like a Goofy: 0 Credy points

'Sattar minute, sattar minute hain tumhare paas.
Shayad tumhari zindagi ke sabse khas sattar minute.
Aaj tum achcha khelo ya bura, ye sattar minute tumhe zindagi bhar yaad rahenge. To kaisa khelna hai aaj main tumhe nahin bataunga, bas itna kahunga ki jao aur ye sattar minute ji bhar ke khel lo.'

22/36

Anti-Monotony: How Credys Sustain Motivation in Repetitive Work

IMAGINE A SALESPERSON chasing the same kind of targets every month, or an IT professional writing code for a single program for months together. Monotonous work can kill people's vigour and energy. As the charm and novelty of the job diminishes with repetition, they can lose interest and motivation. This is where their leader needs to step in and re-energise them to complete the task at hand.

If you secretly aspire to be in a vocation that could change the world, you are not alone. It is a great ambition to have. But the truth of life is that most of us are involved in work of a highly repetitive nature. This repetitiveness, which cuts across industries, professions, hierarchies, and geographies, can cause mental fatigue and stifle creativity. It can turn people into robots.

Good leaders know that repetition is a major cause of boredom and lack of enthusiasm. But they also know that routine work can never be completely free of repetition. So, they take a unique approach – they use the art of 'short-term storytelling' to make monotonous work feel interesting and full of potential.

Short-term storytelling is a great way to beat the tedium of routine. I am calling it *short-term* because it's all about the next week, the next month, or, at the most, the next quarter. And I'm calling it *storytelling* because it's a narrative that can trigger the imagination of your team members.

To put it simply, it is a plan of action presented as a story with a clear beginning, middle, and end. Let's take an example.

Let's say your team follows a monthly sales cycle where they have to meet the same targets month on month. There's every chance they will gradually lose the motivation to give their best. To keep morales high, you must find something unique at the start of each month – a new challenge, an opportunity, a reward – and frame it in a way that gives your team a renewed sense of purpose and a common goal.

This approach is not very different from the motivational speeches given by team captains and coaches before a big game. No wonder we get to see some truly inspired performances after these talks.

That being said, a good leader doesn't just tell a random story. He collects data, studies trends, and backs his arguments with evidence and logic. Once the team is on board, he gets them the resources they will need to succeed. This recharges people. Effectively, the leader acts as a safety net that prevents his team members from falling into the deep, dark hole of feeling sorry for themselves for having to do monotonous work.

I've had the privilege of working with a Credy who strongly believed in the power of short-term storytelling. Every month, he worked hard on data and trends and came up with a 'crystal ball' view of potential outcomes if we followed a certain plan. He began the month with a team meeting where we analysed the previous month's performance and made plans for the current month.

This might sound like regular stuff, but our leader had this magical ability to generate a response from us that was critical to achieving our targets. His deep understanding of the macro and micro factors that affected our performance, his knowhow of individual and common trigger points, his exceptional data analysis and meticulous planning, and, finally, his ability to weave the plan into a compelling story created a synergy that kept us going.

He always opened his story with the current scenario, as in where we stood in terms of resources, opportunities, strengths, and weaknesses. He would then share his plan along with multiple what-if scenarios. This created a sense of excitement. Next, he allocated responsibilities based on our individual interests and skill sets. Finally, he would conclude the discussion by painting a wonderful picture of us as winners if we gave the plan our best shot. The entire exercise took only a couple of hours, but it took him two to three days to prepare for it.

Quite naturally, working with this leader never felt like work but more like an adventurous trek where we all knew the route, the terrain, the challenges, and the supplies we needed for the climb.

Let me share an incident where he painted a promising future scenario to motivate us to reach the finish line. We were recovering from a very tiring end to the month, having chased our targets every hour and every day of the final week. This meant having the same telephone conversations over and over with our dealer-partners and repeated visits to their offices in the heat of June. We were exhausted mentally and physically, but before we could blink, there came July.

As usual, our leader called for a team meeting. After revealing the analytic and strategic parts of his plan for the month, he added, 'These sales numbers will be the highest numbers ever achieved in July by any team in our company's history. If we meet these targets, our inventory stocks will drop to an all-time low. With the festival season coming up, there is going to be a surge in enquiries. This means demand for all our products will surpass the supply. That would be an ideal situation for us. We will hit a historic milestone in July and still exceed our targets for August, September, and October.'

He was right. A low inventory combined with demand outstripping supply meant that we could have an easier time once we met our numbers for July. Using a compelling narrative, he had successfully sold us the opportunity to break a record and earn the reward of a comfortable three months ahead.

An action plan presented in this way achieves two goals. First, it tells your team why that plan is the best plan. Second, once they are convinced with the *why* part, getting them to follow the *what needs to be done* part becomes easier. Results still cannot be guaranteed, but hundred per cent effort is guaranteed.

Credys understand that not every task is a marathon. More often, it's a short sprint that needs a concentrated burst of effort, where people are expected to put up their best show in a short span of time. So they create an environment where everyone wants to contribute, learn, and excel.

On the other hand, Goofys have neither the intent to align their team to a common goal nor the calibre to communicate targets in an exciting manner. Instead, they resort to hollow josh talks, which, as we all know, rarely move the needle of motivation. Moreover, since Goofys don't get involved in the planning process, they have a volley of questions when approached for resources or support. This causes unnecessary delays.

Goofys fail to cultivate a sense of purpose in their team because they lack a sense of purpose themselves. This is why, in *Goofiland*, work often feel like a burden, a sense of achievement is sorely missing, and results elude the team.

I had a leader who was a living example of this behaviour. His team discussions only revolved around the targets he wanted us to achieve, with no guidance on how we should proceed. Worse, these targets were never his own brainchild but mere numbers passed down by his seniors.

This Goofy refused to see that we were trapped in a monotonous process, bored and completely out of ideas. But far from motivating us, he never missed a chance to remind us that we were obliged to give our best simply because we were being paid. His transactional approach took away any little zeal we had left. Our performance continued to decline month after month and never recovered as long as he was our leader.

To get things done, you should know how to tap into the individual and collective passions of your team. You should know what inspires them to bring their best game to the table. And with this knowledge, you should paint a vivid picture of the short-term future, showing how today's efforts will lead to better tomorrows. This combination of personal passion and collective energy will create a mission-like environment with no place for boredom or monotony.

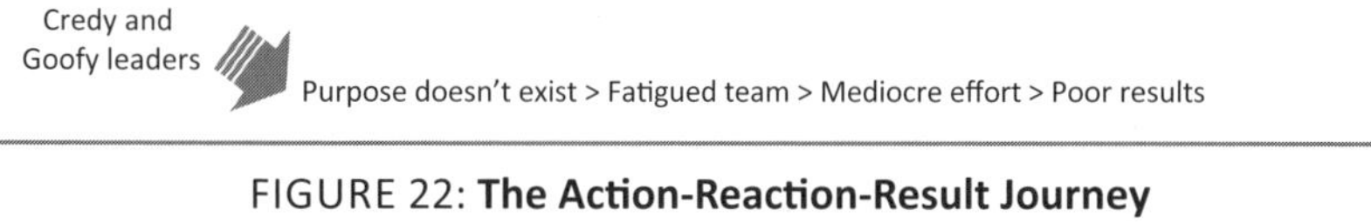

FIGURE 22: **The Action-Reaction-Result Journey**

Key Takeaways

- At the start of every performance period, do your homework and create an aspirational plan for your team, especially if their work is repetitive in nature. This homework should be twofold – a thorough analysis of data, trends, and targets on one hand and an in-depth understanding of individual and team aspirations on the other. When you marry these two sets of knowledge into a plan, you will have completed your homework.
- Next comes the task of weaving a magical story around your plan that will inspire people to commit to it with body, mind, and soul. Here are a few ideas:
    - Explain how hard work in the current week, month, or quarter will set the tone for the next performance period and make it a walk in the park.
    - Talk about how exceptional performance can help your team outshine the competition.
    - Frame the period as an opportunity to recover from earlier losses.
    - Bring renewed focus on a product or service.
- Lastly, remind yourself that you're dealing with people, not machines. Make an effort to learn the art of short-term storytelling. Once you ace it, crafting inspiring narratives will become effortless with time.

Self-Evaluation

Reflect on your ability to keep your team energised throughout a performance period. Evaluate yourself with the following questions:

- Are you aware that some or all of the work done by your team may be boring or uninspiring due to its repetitive or rigorous nature?
- Do you believe you must go beyond transactional relationships and help your team members feel a deeper connection to their work?

Are you able to look into data, do a SWOT-like analysis, strategise, and present it to your team in an engaging manner?

Now, give yourself Credy Points based on your behaviour in the above context. Pick the appropriate option:

- ◯ Always behave like a Credy: 10 Credy points
- ◯ Mostly behave like a Credy: 7 Credy points
- ◯ Sometimes behave like a Credy, sometimes like a Goofy: 4 Credy points
- ◯ Always behave like a Goofy: 0 Credy points

'Har bachche ki apni khoobi hoti hai,
apni kaabiliyat hoti hai, apni chahat hoti hai.'

23/36

Learning and Development: How Goofys Prevent Progress

YOU'VE PROBABLY SEEN a lot of organisations where any effort to enhance people's knowledge or skills is seen as a burden rather than a necessity. This is often because upskilling people is a long-term goal that clashes with the demands of daily work. Trainings, conferences, seminars, and workshops need time, which is always in short supply. But an even bigger problem is when leaders see development activities as a waste of time. This myopic vision robs people of the opportunity to grow and learn, leaving them stuck with stale knowledge, redundant skills, low productivity, poor output, and inability to cope with change. In my view, it's outright selfish for a leader to keep using people without having an eye on their development. It reeks of a use-and-throw mentality.

When people join the workforce, their formal education ends but their learning continues. With the macro and micro ecosystems changing constantly, there is always something new to learn. While every professional has a responsibility to stay up-to-date in their field, it is their leader who needs to actively create opportunities for them to upskill and upgrade.

Some leaders are pro-development by nature. They have a genuine desire to help others learn and grow, and this reflects in the knowledge, skills, and confidence levels of their team members.

I once worked with a Credy leader who was genuinely interested in the continuous professional development (CPD) of his team. Every few months, he had one-on-one meetings with us to discuss our individual developmental plans and help us pick the right training programmes. He then worked with HR to organise these sessions.

Unlike many of his Goofy colleagues, he picked trainings that matched our specific needs. Those of us struggling with communication, for example, were encouraged to sign up for communication workshops. Those transitioning to projects were asked to train in a project management methodology like Agile.

Some leaders saw these training activities as a waste of time, but for our leader, the new skills we gained adequately compensated for the time we spent away from work.

Soon enough, we came to be known as a team with skills that were often lacking in others. Many of us transformed into powerhouses of specialist knowledge, and other teams regularly sought our help with specialised tasks.

When a leader is genuinely involved in developing people, it builds competencies and makes the organisation a learning organisation. It also builds morale – when people see themselves being developed by design, they feel inspired to excel in their work.

Goofys, on the other hand, see no value in training or mentorship. Forget about proactively organising CPD activities, they try to block any door that could lead to better prospects for their subordinates. This behaviour has multiple reasons – fear of having team members who are more skilled or knowledgeable than oneself, the misconception that development activities disrupt day-to-day work, or a desire to keep people on a tight leash so they won't be eligible for higher-order roles.

I had a Goofy leader who sent us for trainings only when he was questioned by his own leader about the shortfall in our training targets. Even then, he would send us to random workshops just to achieve the bare minimum training days. When we returned, he never wanted to know what we had learned. Instead, he would ask inconsequential questions like 'How was the food and accommodation?', making us feel like we had been on a paid holiday by his majesty's blessings.

Being young and naive, we followed this Goofy's orders without question, not realising that we were being forced to learn skills we didn't need. Far from helping us grow, he wasted our time and energy and made us lose confidence in our abilities. Many of us hit a plateau in our learning curves and lived with the frustration of being left behind.

Thankfully, I've worked with more Credys than Goofys. What I've learned is that a leader's approach to developing people says a lot about his *Crediniyat*. Credys don't just encourage CPD; they use it to build high-performing teams armed with superior skills and knowledge. You will find many Credys with multiple aces up their sleeve in the form of super skilled team members. In contrast, Goofys lead outdated teams with no edge over competition.

Having said that, it would be wrong to blame people's stale knowledge or incompetence entirely on their leaders. I've met many professionals who have no interest in upgrading themselves. More surprisingly, they don't seem to care how this attitude affects their career growth. The damage is even more evident when their leader shares the same mindset. There are exceptions, of course, where despite their Goofy leader's indifference, people choose to invest in themselves, but such cases are rare.

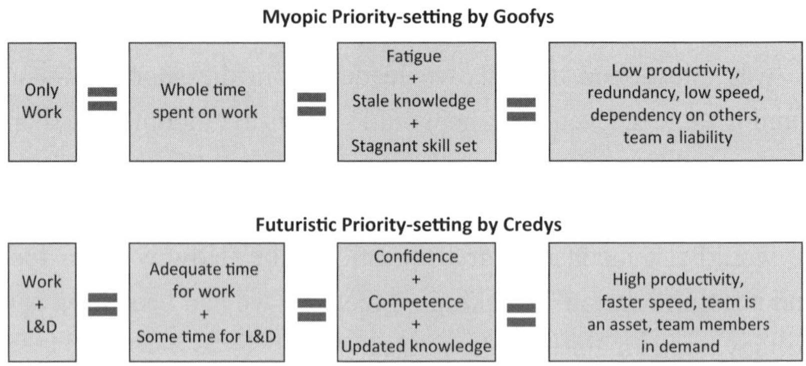

FIGURE 23: **Consequences of Goofy's Myopic Vision vs Credy's Futuristic Vision**

Key Takeaways

- As a leader, only you can make room for your team members to get upskilled. Be a leader who is building a team and not just completing tasks.
- It is both your duty and in your best interest to keep your team updated before they get outdated. If you don't lead on this front, you will have team members who are feeding you stale knowledge that has lost its relevance.
- Some of the biggest learning and development happens through your own interactions with your team. Make a deliberate effort to learn about the aspirations, career goals, and future vision of your team members.

Self-Evaluation

Reflect on how positive and proactive you are in creating development opportunities for your team. Evaluate yourself with the following questions:

- Do you believe that upskilling your team members strengthens the team as a whole?
- Do you see training activities as a hindrance to work?
- Do you think carefully before nominating someone for a training programme?
- Do you see CPD as an investment or an expense?
- Do you proactively chalk out the developmental journeys of your team members?

Now, give yourself Credy Points based on your behaviour in the above context. Pick the appropriate option:

- ○ Always behave like a Credy: 10 Credy points
- ○ Mostly behave like a Credy: 7 Credy points
- ○ Sometimes behave like a Credy, sometimes like a Goofy: 4 Credy points
- ○ Always behave like a Goofy: 0 Credy points

'Bhagwan ke bharose mat baithiye,
kaa pata Bhagwan humare bharose baitha ho.'

24/36

Anticipating Opportunities: How Credys Stay Ahead of the Pack

Great leaders are able to look beyond the obvious, comprehend the unsaid, foresee opportunities that are not immediately apparent, and then take actions that advance their team forward. While their team focuses on routine tasks, these leaders watch out for out-of-the-ordinary situations and come up with a winning plan to capitalise on them. Credys consistently take advantage of such opportunities, but Goofys almost always miss out on them. This is either because they fail to predict such scenarios or because they simply choose not to act. Here, we are talking about a leader's role in seizing opportunities within the internal operating environment, not the external one. It is about taking advantage of the events and changes that happen within every organisation. A leader's credibility grows or diminishes in direct proportion to whether he is in the driving seat or is being driven by these developments.

One of the foremost traits of a Credy leader is a sharp awareness of his environment. This leads to unboxing of potential opportunities and even hidden challenges, enabling him to strategise much ahead of the curve.

Opportunities come in many forms. It can be a meeting with the senior leadership, an important conference, or the formation of a new department or business vertical. Credys don't attend these events as mere spectators; they step up and take charge so they can capitalise on the situation for the benefit of their team. To achieve this, they take two clear actions: they find an opportunity in such events and then come up with a plan to encash the opportunity.

For example, in a meeting with senior leaders to discuss a pre-defined agenda, a Credy leader might use the forum to raise a pending issue affecting his team, highlight a recent achievement that went unnoticed, or push for a proposal that needs approval. For this, he would first have to ensure that the particular issue is included in the meeting's agenda. This needs a great deal of planning and foresight.

Opportunities like these don't come often, but when they do, Credys make use of them while ensuring there is no dissonance with other stakeholders. I had a hands-on experience of this with one of my leaders. We had a visit coming up from our topmost management, who were arriving with a full entourage and a packed schedule.

Until then, I had always seen leaders stick to the agenda set by the visit coordinator. Suggesting a change never occurred to them, and even when it did, they could never gather the courage to propose it. Protocol was followed without question, no matter what.

But our leader had a different plan. We had just bagged a marquee project, but to proceed, we needed budget approvals that could only be sanctioned by the highest leadership. The standard approval process generally took four to six weeks, but our leader wasn't willing to wait that long. He asked us to prepare a compelling proposal while he worked with the visiting leaders' administrative staff to get a time slot for the presentation.

His efforts paid off. The presentation went extremely well and the proposal was passed with minimal resistance. It also set the tone for the rest of the visit. I'm not sure what the top brass thought of our leader before, but this meeting clearly cemented his image as a champion for the organisation's and the team's cause. For the record, the country leadership mentioned our presentation on multiple occasions as something to learn from.

In sharp contrast, one of my Goofy leaders was so laid-back that he had no idea of the changes happening in the ecosystem. He even struggled with his core responsibilities, so expecting anything more from him was out of the question. One incident still stands out in my mind.

Like many businesses of that time, our organisation was trying to become more tech-savvy. A new initiative called 'Project Digitalisation' was launched, and a dedicated team was set up to automate manual data entry. Every department was given a timeframe to submit their requirements, but our Goofy leader kept procrastinating until the last moment. Not only did we miss the deadline, he did not even ask for an extension.

Not surprisingly, the digital team soon had their hands full with a year's worth of work from other departments. As a result, we had to struggle with manual processes for a large part of that year. Our Goofy leader's lethargy and indifference crippled the progress of the entire team.

We later learned that he was reprimanded by senior management for always being critical of manual processes only to miss the opportunity for automation when it was served to him on a platter.

In any organisation, leaders and teams that excel are the ones that can outshine others through basic qualities like hard work and discipline topped with some out-of-the-box thinking, some ahead-of-the-curve actions, the ability to seize first-mover advantage, and a few clever moves.

This is where Credys and Goofys lead differently. With a minimalist approach to work and no zeal to explore or reinvent the future, Goofys don't care to challenge the status-quo. Their moronic and lazy approach robs their team of any chance to outperform others. As a result, they slowly get pushed out of the organisation's mainstream, where the major positive disruption and progress are happening.

Credys are, by nature, forward-looking design thinkers. They don't sit, wait, and watch perpetually; they think and act to create positive situations for themselves and their teams.

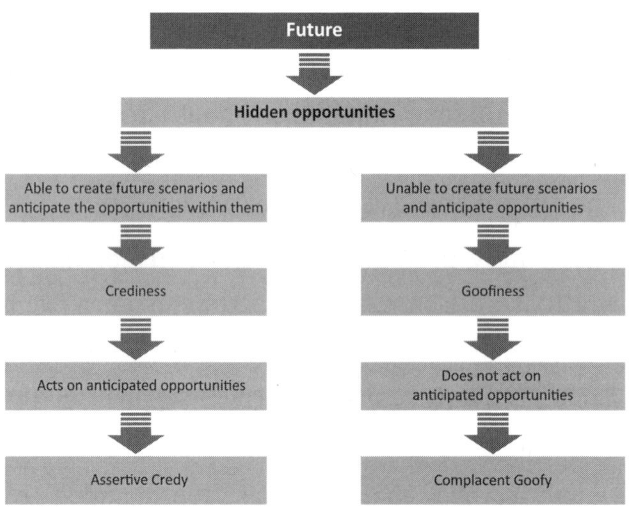

FIGURE 24: **The Algorithm of Anticipating Opportunities**

Key Takeaways

- As a leader, you have to be on your toes and stick out your neck for opportunities. You have to anticipate the future and prepare for it.
- While your team focuses on today's work and this week's tasks, you have the duty and privilege to zoom out and look at the bigger picture.
- Ultimately, your vision and foresight will define whether you and your team are in the driving seat or are just being driven by circumstances.

Self-Evaluation

Reflect on how well you can anticipate opportunities and how nimble-footed you are in taking advantage of them. Evaluate yourself with the following questions:

- Are you able to foresee opportunities in your ecosystem?
- Do you recall a situation where you proactively seized an opportunity or thwarted a threat to your team?
- Do you consider it your responsibility to plan ahead while your team members focus on their routine tasks?

Now, give yourself Credy Points based on your behaviour in the above context. Pick the appropriate option:

- ○ Always behave like a Credy: 10 Credy points
- ○ Mostly behave like a Credy: 7 Credy points
- ○ Sometimes behave like a Credy, sometimes like a Goofy: 4 Credy points
- ○ Always behave like a Goofy: 0 Credy points

'Bachcha kabil bano, kabil...
kamyabi to sali jhak maar ke peeche bhagegi.'

25/36

Mastering Feedback

EVERY LEADER WANTS his team to become stronger and better with passage of time. Similarly, every team member has a fundamental need to improve and grow. But this ambition can be realised only when both parties know what needs to improve and how to go about it. This makes exchange of feedback a critical part of their relationship. Credy leaders use feedback to help their team members reach the next level of expertise. They are bold enough to show people the mirror, even when the reflection may not be so great. Goofys, on the other hand, avoid giving honest feedback. They either have no idea what needs improvement or are not articulate enough to give constructive feedback. Worse, some Goofys use unjustified criticism to vent their frustration at people they dislike. Leaders who master the art of thoughtful and practical feedback earn lasting respect and devotion, but those who knowingly choose stupidity over wisdom struggle to command even basic respect from their teams.

At the end of an annual performance cycle, most organisations conduct performance reviews where people receive feedback from their leaders on their performance and behaviour. This feedback forms the basis for salary increments, promotions, performance-linked bonuses, transfers, and so on. In short, a lot depends on these year-end reviews. Considering the sensitivity of the process, it needs to be handled with great care.

In general, people are resistant to feedback that points out their weaknesses or areas of improvement. But if the same feedback is backed with specific incidents and data and delivered with objectivity, it sinks in sooner or later. It may initially cause dissatisfaction or disagreement, and may even make the leader look like a villain, but if given with the right intent, it eventually leads to acceptance and respect for the leader.

So how should leaders go about tracking and analysing the performance of their team members? Let me share a fantastic approach followed by one of my Credy leaders.

First, to be objective in his year-end appraisals, he maintained a detailed record of each of his direct reportees, including any exceptional achievements, obstacles faced, challenges overcome, targets missed, and behaviour during crisis. He documented these details in a diary he called 'CID' (Critical Incident Diary). Second, he believed in providing immediate feedback throughout the year. This gave people a chance to improve and course-correct as needed.

This approach added so much credibility to his performance reviews that we readily accepted the ratings and gradings we were given. Furthermore, this Credy did not believe in the 'recency effect' – the notion that the last two or three months of a performance cycle accurately reflect someone's overall performance.

Take my own example. After two great years in the company, I was confident that I would get a high rating in my third year as well, especially given my stupendous performance in the three months leading up to the review. With this notion, I walked into the meeting expecting an 'Outstanding' rating.

As always, my leader started on a positive note. He appreciated my contributions to the business, my positive mindset, and my professionalism. Then he asked me to reflect on the lack of focus I had displayed during the first nine months of the year. He helped me see that I had been overconfident and had made some avoidable mistakes. He backed his observations with specific examples that made it clear that I had not performed as well as I believed.

As you can see, while being generous with his praise, my leader was equally upfront about where I stood that year. I received a downgraded rating, which was hard to accept at first. I felt angry, sad, and frustrated for many days. But the more I reflected on my leader's feedback, the more I realised that every word he said was true. Eventually, I accepted the feedback and resolved never to repeat those mistakes.

This is how my leader inspired me to give my best all year round. With his constructive feedback, he created an environment where I felt comfortable approaching him for guidance without any fear of judgement.

Timid Goofys, on the other hand, can cross all limits of stupidity when it comes to giving individual feedback. I saw a classic display of this goofiness when a fellow leader, who had over a hundred direct or indirect reportees, announced that from that year onwards his annual performance ratings were going to be based on '360-degree feedback'. In other words, people would be rated not just by their supervisors but also by their peers and subordinates.

The decision reflected this Goofy's spineless style of leadership. Since he had neither the right framework for year-end reviews nor the guts to give unbiased feedback, he conveniently chose to hide behind the garb of 360-degree feedback. The height of his stupidity was that he made the announcement near the end of the performance cycle, as if shouting at the top of his voice, 'Surprise, surprise!'

The short notice caught everyone off guard and caused a state of panic. What was supposed to be a fair assessment of performance turned into a popularity contest, where your future in the company depended on the opinions of co-workers who might not even know you well.

When the stakes are this high, impressing and influencing your colleagues is the only way to win. It puts pressure on you to be good at politics rather than being good at your job. The aftermath of this disastrous experiment was a complete loss of Goofy's credibility. People wholeheartedly rejected him as their leader. Even fresh graduates, who had barely completed a year in the organisation, lost faith in his leadership.

In all fairness, the 360-degree feedback model might have some merit when your goal is to help people understand how they are perceived by their colleagues. But under no circumstances should it be used to calculate annual ratings, salary increments, or bonuses. People work in a chain of command, and only their immediate supervisor can accurately assess their performance.

Moreover, performance cannot just be weighed against numbers; there is always an element of subjectivity. As a leader, it is your duty to monitor your team members throughout the performance cycle. Chronicle the hits and misses, considering factors like circumstances, unforeseen events, difficulties faced, available resources, and any ambiguities in delegation. Only then can you make a fair assessment.

Finally, remember that even the most comprehensive assessment is only half the work done. The other half is about how well you articulate the facts and findings, because it's not just what you say but how you say it that will make people accept your feedback, maybe not in front of you, but in their hearts for sure.

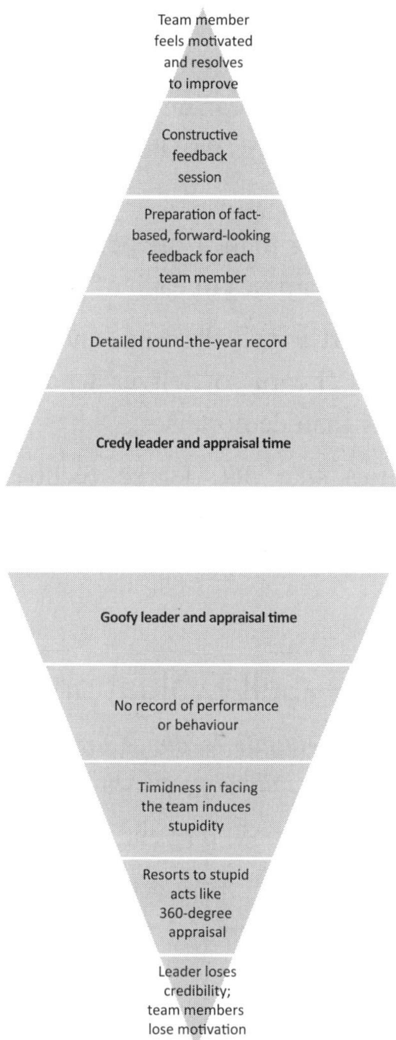

FIGURE 25: **The Appraisal Pyramids**

Key Takeaways

- Year-end performance reviews can make or break careers, or at least impact people's growth in the organisation, so approach the process with a rational mind.
- Don't save things for year-end reviews. If you give honest feedback throughout the year, and back your observations with facts, your year-end ratings will be readily accepted by most of your subordinates.
- Use a solid framework to measure performance, and document noteworthy hits and misses of each of your direct reportees.
- Have a brave heart to tell the truth and a kind heart to help construct careers. Learn to deliver feedback in a way that empowers rather than demoralises.
- Avoid stupidities like 360-degree feedback. An objective year-end review and 360-degree feedback are like chalk and cheese – they look similar but have completely different purposes.

Self-Evaluation

Reflect on how well you handle feedback and appraisals as a leader. Evaluate yourself with the following questions:

- Do you set clear expectations for your team members at the start of the year?
- Do you ensure that your annual reviews are based only on actual performance?
- Do you consciously avoid the recency effect when providing feedback or assessing performance?
- Do you record critical incidents throughout the year?

Now, give yourself Credy Points based on your behaviour in the above context. Pick the appropriate option:

- ○ Always behave like a Credy: 10 Credy points
- ○ Mostly behave like a Credy: 7 Credy points
- ○ Sometimes behave like a Credy, sometimes like a Goofy: 4 Credy points
- ○ Always behave like a Goofy: 0 Credy points

'Moonche ho to Nathulal jaisi hon... warna na hon.'

'Mogambo khush hua!'

26/36

Fake Praise vs Authentic Appreciation

WHEN IT COMES to motivating a person or a group, there is no better alternative to the power of appreciation. It is both a leader's duty and privilege to use this power to keep his team inspired and energised. But with this power comes responsibility – the responsibility to be a genuine appreciator. Regardless of the receiver's rank, age, or experience, genuineness in appreciation makes all the difference. A few honest words of appreciation are a zillion times more effective than superficial praise offered in a grand ceremony. In short, the power of appreciation can be harnessed or wasted based on one critical factor: genuineness.

Appreciation is a superpower that is used to its fullest by Credys but completely wasted by Goofys. Most Goofys ignore a fundamental rule of appreciation: it has to be authentic. Appreciating people just for the sake of it never does the job. What truly makes a difference is being transparent, sincere, and intentional with your words.

Lately, there has been a strange trend in organisations. In the name of 'employee engagement' or 'rewards and recognition', even the most routine achievements are celebrated with grand gestures. No one likes to hear this, but rituals like cake-cutting, clapping, and cheering for routine tasks don't motivate anyone – except maybe the baker who supplied the cake!

Worse, even mediocre performance is sometimes celebrated with great fanfare, all in the garb of motivating people at any cost. While I'm not against finding positives in the face of failure, celebrating non-performance is a different matter altogether.

I have worked with leaders who had a compulsive need to find something to applaud. At times, the reason was so miniscule that even those being recognised ate the cake with a heavy heart. I remember an instance where, even though we had achieved less than 50 per cent of our monthly target, our leader was full of praise for us, all because we had not taken a single day off that month!

Leaders who consider it their duty to cheer for everything lose their credibility as genuine appreciators. They are seen as weak and eager to please. In fact, I have seen many good performers not want to be recognised by their Goofy leaders. Yes, you read that right. Being appreciated by a fool is counterproductive, as it makes the onlookers form a similar Goofy image of you. At any rate, not being appreciated is any day better than receiving hollow praise just for doing your job, which sorely diminishes the value of appreciation.

Another absurd celebration I recall was held to mark the release of a newspaper advertisement by our department. The whole thing was befuddling for many reasons. First, our office published at least half a dozen print ads every month, so there was nothing special about this one. Second, it was an expense with no guarantee of results. Third, the entire creative process was outsourced to an external agency, so our only real contribution to the campaign was giving some 'high-level' directions. To top it off, our sales actually declined after the ad was released. While I'm not directly attributing the drop in sales to the ad, it certainly made no positive impact on the business.

Nevertheless, we had a big celebration, all because a bunch of us thought we had created a brilliant advertisement, conveniently ignoring the fact that it had turned out to be an utter failure.

Another common goofed-up scenario is when leaders hold big gatherings to celebrate good results, but forget to acknowledge the actual people or the exact reasons behind the success. In their typical Goofy style, they indiscriminately applaud one and all, missing the golden opportunity to recognise those who deserve it the most.

Whether it's a team gathering, a town hall, or a social event, you cannot just announce the results, offer a generic thank-you, and say, 'We will do a deep dive later.' Please do the deep dive first and then make the speech. Present a clear diagnosis of the results, the insights gained, and the future course of action. Most importantly, say your thanks loud and clear to those behind the win. Appreciate the specific actions that brought success, rather than making it sound like an outcome of luck, fluke, or circumstance.

I had the pleasure of working with a Credy leader who had mastered the art of genuine appreciation. After every success, he would analyse the results in depth and share his findings with all concerned. When appreciating our efforts, he did not just acknowledge the outcome but the entire journey that led to it. His manner of appreciation resonated with everyone. The cake tasted sweeter, the applause sounded more real, motivation soared, and self-esteem grew by leaps. We looked forward to these sessions with him.

On the flip side, compulsive and excessive praise is a sure-fire way to lose your credibility. If the goal is to motivate people, a simple but authentic 'Well done!' is better received than a beautiful and expensive trophy awarded for a mediocre show. Meaningful and selective appreciation will build your reputation as an astute judge of good work and inspire your team to strive for your recognition.

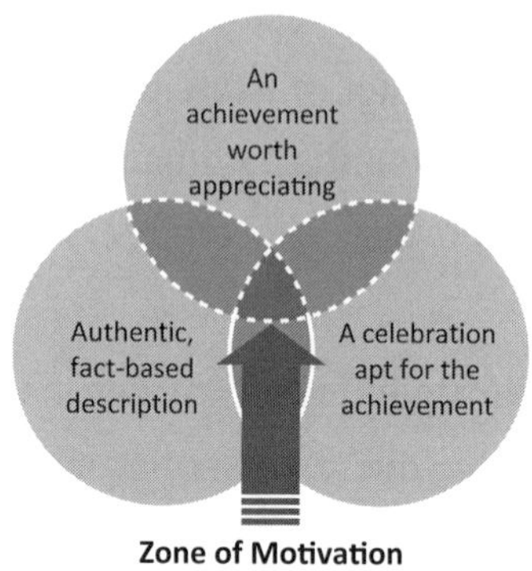

FIGURE 26: **Zone of Motivation**

Key Takeaways

- Believe me, your team members are more mature than you think. They know the difference between real and fake appreciation, so treat them with the respect they deserve. In other words, be a real admirer, not a charitable one.
- Excessive or insincere praise not only tarnishes your reputation but also fails to make anyone happy.
- Be mindful in your appreciation. Set high standards, choose your words carefully, and give credit to those who have earned it.

Self-Evaluation

Reflect on how genuine and balanced you are when appreciating your team members. Evaluate yourself with the following questions:

- Do you agree that *genuineness* is the keyword when it comes to appreciation?
- Do you actively look for opportunities to recognise and applaud your team members?
- Are you able to suppress the urge to appreciate just to please someone?

Now, give yourself Credy Points based on your behaviour in the above context. Pick the appropriate option:

- ○ Always behave like a Credy: 10 Credy points
- ○ Mostly behave like a Credy: 7 Credy points
- ○ Sometimes behave like a Credy, sometimes like a Goofy: 4 Credy points
- ○ Always behave like a Goofy: 0 Credy points

'Taqat toh gainda bhi lagata hai...
lekin sher lagata hai taqat aur technique dono...
sher ban'na hai, gainda nahi.'

27/36

Logic, Research, and Experience: Three Pillars of a Solid Action Plan

WHAT WOULD YOU think of your leader if he asks you to go on a mission without divulging any details about it? It's not like there is any secrecy to be maintained, but your leader just didn't find it necessary to brief you, or maybe he didn't want to do the hard work to make the plan sound compelling to you. Similarly, imagine someone telling you to jump from the fourth floor while giving no other information versus them telling you to jump because there's a fire in the building and that is the only safe exit. They also reassure you that there's a team of firefighters standing below for your safe landing. Which of these people would you trust?

In uncertain situations, Credy leaders use logic, research, and the wealth of their experience to validate their instincts. This quality helps them make sound decisions even in the most unprecedented circumstances. They know that they may not always be correct, but they are definitely not confused. This sense of conviction in a leader is crucial for unified action by his team.

Credys believe in creating a solid plan based on certain assumptions, some facts, and some logic. When they put forward the plan to their team, they explain the opportunity, the challenges, the risks, required resources, and expectations from each team member. They also share a contingency plan in case the original plan doesn't work. This gets them complete commitment from their team to execute the plan to the best of their abilities. In other words, Credys don't just pass orders, they *Credify* them.

One of my leaders followed exactly this approach. Whenever he rolled out a strategic plan, he also shared the assumptions, risks, black boxes (areas of uncertainty), and what-if scenarios. This groundwork changed the entire complexion of his strategic meetings. It added credibility to his plans and generated an instant buy-in from us.

I also had a Goofy leader who had only one thing to say when presenting a plan of action: 'There is no clear right or wrong in any plan, so let's do this and we will see.' Convenient? Yes. Logical? No. But with his limited ability to analyse trends and data, this was the best he could do. Not just this, he would come to strategic meetings with randomly conceived plans and, to hide his incompetence and casual approach, he never even faintly tried to explain the rationale behind the plan. What-if scenarios were completely ignored.

When some of us questioned his plan – not to challenge him but to understand why it did not look convincing – he responded with the same rant: 'There's no right or wrong, so let's just go ahead.'

According to this Goofy, he had come up with the best possible plan and now it was our duty to make it successful. This was his way of taking an anticipatory bail in case things went south.

When a leader skips the groundwork, makes arbitrary decisions, and avoids open discussion, the result is a weak plan that has little appeal for his team. To them, it is never 'our' plan but always 'his' plan. As a result, the seed of underperformance is sowed at the start itself.

Naturally, when the leader himself is only half-interested or half-sure, when he is focused more on creating an escape route for himself than on developing a failproof plan, his team too will work half-heartedly.

Agreed, not every plan can be modelled with precision; there will always be grey areas. But I have seen the same plans receive very different reactions and levels of commitment based on how they were presented.

Goofys love to shove half-baked plans down people's throats, with the rider that 'there is no absolute right or wrong', but most such plans die in the nascent stage itself. Or they die soon afterwards, when cross-functional debates take centre stage and stakeholders ask some hard questions. Even if a weak plan gets past this stage, it is executed with low interest and low confidence by the team.

Call it luck or mindset, but if you start with doubts, you are bound to face obstacles on your path. This is why Credy leaders do all they can to make their plans as failproof as possible. No leader has a crystal ball to look into the future, but what Credys do have is the common sense to do thorough research and find unknown factors that could affect the success of their plan. Armed with this knowledge, they confidently choose a course of action. Their belief in the plan motivates their team to go all out and make it a roaring success, which includes ensuring buy-in from stakeholders both inside and outside the organisation.

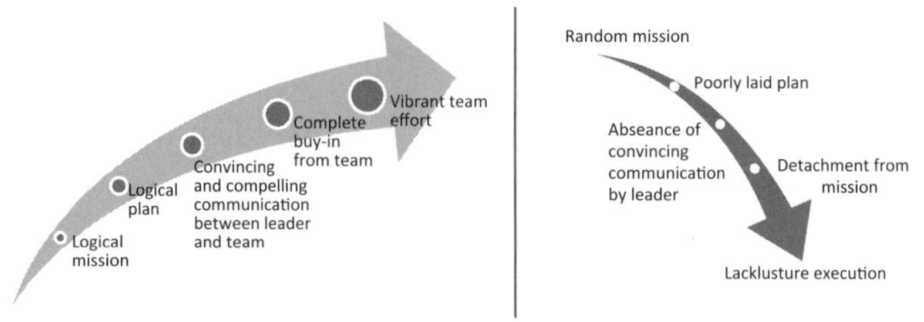

FIGURE 27: **Design for Success vs Design for Failure**

Key Takeaways

- Before you share a strategic plan with your team, do your homework to make sure it sounds credible and doable. This prep work is important to generate confidence in your move.
- Data and research are important, but they are not the only convincing factors at your disposal. If that were the case, nothing disruptive would ever be achieved. It has to be the right mix of data, research, gut feeling, and emotions.
- You cannot expect wholehearted commitment from your team unless you are fully convinced of a plan's potential. Be clear why you want to follow a certain path.
- Lastly, never say that there is no definitive right or wrong – people know that already. By saying this about your own plan, you are only eroding your credibility and entering the Goofy zone.

Self-Evaluation

Reflect on how well you use logic, research, and your past experience when developing action plans for your team. Evaluate yourself with the following questions:

- Do you do the hard work that goes into creating a solid plan of action for your team?

- Are you good at analysing trends and data for building what-if scenarios?
- Do you try to remove ambiguity from your plans as much as possible?

Now, give yourself Credy Points based on your behaviour in the above context. Pick the appropriate option:

- ○ Always behave like a Credy: 10 Credy points
- ○ Mostly behave like a Credy: 7 Credy points
- ○ Sometimes behave like a Credy, sometimes like a Goofy: 4 Credy points
- ○ Always behave like a Goofy: 0 Credy points

'Picture abhi baaki hai mere dost!'

28/36

Igniting Aspirations for Long-Term Success

HAVE YOU EVER been denied a long-due and well-deserved promotion at work? Or seen it happen to someone you know? Almost everyone faces this situation at some point, and when they do, it breaks their morale and momentum. A leader's credibility is tested by how he handles the setback and brings the team member back into the groove. Credible leaders do this without resorting to false promises or hollow statements. Nor do they use threat or fear to get the focus back. They are genuinely interested in the long-term career of their team members, so they handle the issue with great care and passion.

A typical employer-employee relationship is generally transactional in nature – employees complete a pre-defined set of tasks and receive compensation in return. In theory, this arrangement should work out perfectly, but that rarely happens in real life. That's because people are not vending machines that will give what is asked of them in exchange of money. Regardless of the policies or culture of an organisation, a leader's relationship with his team can never be purely transactional. People care about their professional growth, and they expect their leader to be equally interested in helping them grow.

In this context, long-term storytelling can be described as the art of predicting or designing a team member's future for the next few years. A leader does this by creating what-if scenarios that show the person *what* will follow *if* they take certain actions, where *what* denotes their aspirations and *if* denotes their performance. This motivates people and helps them recover from both minor setbacks and major debacles like a missed promotion.

In this day and age, people want a leader who will guide and mentor them and not just use them for commercial purposes. Credy leaders understand this well. They know that beyond a certain point, people work for their personal ambitions and not just to make money. It could be a bigger role, a new title, vertical or lateral promotion, transfer to a preferred location, or something else – there is something beyond money that drives people to perform.

Credys also know that people are most productive when they know that they are on the path of growth. Accordingly, they take the time to understand the individual needs, wants, aspirations, training gaps, and personal challenges of each team member. Using this knowledge, they help people figure out a long-term career path that aligns with their professional and personal goals.

I learned the art of long-term storytelling from a Credy leader of mine. Whenever he found it appropriate or necessary, he would draw you into a conversation that made you feel like he understood your deepest thoughts and aspirations. He had a remarkable ability to connect your current role with future trends in the field, which left you convinced that you were already on the path to your next big opportunity. This made you want to excel in your work, knowing that it would pave the way to your ultimate career goal.

I remember a conversation we had one afternoon on our way to a vendor's factory. I had just been denied a promotion I was sure to get, whereas many of my peers had been promoted. I was very frustrated, but since my leader wasn't part of the promotions committee, I had decided not to talk to him about it. But that day, after some initial chitchat, he broached the topic himself.

To my surprise, he said he believed I was more deserving of a promotion than many who had been promoted. He even explained the rationale behind his opinion, which put me at ease and I decided to open up about how I was feeling.

It felt good to be heard, but as I replayed the conversation in my head that night, I realised that my leader's real intention wasn't just to give me a platform to vent. Once my guard was down, he steered the conversation to assure me of two things. First, in a career that was to span decades, missing one promotion was not the end of the world. Second, how well I was preparing for my next big role was far more important than dwelling on the missed opportunity.

His second observation felt as if he had read my mind. Though I was unhappy about not being promoted, deep down, I knew I needed more time in my current role to know the game better. I needed to be thoroughly prepared for a higher-order position that would demand much more out of me.

Looking back, that conversation with my leader – one that now seems thoroughly prepared and carefully timed – changed the way I looked at promotions. He helped me realise the importance of consolidating my existing knowledge before taking the next big leap. According to him, it was better to wait for the right time than to rush forward and find yourself grossly underprepared. He shared examples from his own career, specifically how spending the right amount of time in each role had made him fundamentally strong as a leader. 'Fast-track growth is attractive,' he said, 'but it can also become the reason for fast-track failure and burnout.'

His words proved right in the coming years, as I found myself in one meaningful role after another. And just as he had predicted, my deep experience proved invaluable in each of those positions.

This experience also taught me an important lesson in leadership: even if it wasn't your decision or action that demotivated a team member, it is still in your interest to address the problem. The elephant in the room should be dealt with as soon as possible. An honest and uplifting conversation can flip the way someone looks at a situation. What you must have is an understanding of their unique personality and aspirations. Only then will you be able to weave a credible long-term story to inspire them.

On the flip side, one of my Goofy leaders made a complete mess of a similar scenario. In this case, a capable member of my team was denied a promotion by our promotions panel. He was one of our brightest, and I didn't want this setback to become a reason for him to quit. I had a round of discussions with him, but then decided to involve my own boss to be sure of a positive outcome.

To my disappointment, Goofy's response was shocking to say the least. Instead of helping to defuse the situation, he asked me to compile a list of the smallest non-achievements of this team member so we could corner him and prove that he didn't deserve the promotion.

This Goofy didn't have the courage, aptitude, or intent to have an honest conversation with a skip-level junior – a conversation that could have healed his fresh wound of being denied a promotion and motivated him to give his best in the next cycle. While I rued the lost opportunity, my team member left the organisation shortly afterwards.

My leader's manipulative tactics harmed everyone involved, but their biggest casualty was Goofy himself. After this incident, his credibility went into a negative spiral. He lost his reputation as a leader with mettle, mistrust started brewing between us, and the atmosphere turned more and more transactional.

This only goes to show that leaders who have a use-and-discard mentality don't go a long way and are bound to stumble and fall at some point.

In summary, your subordinates may be doing great work, but if they don't see it benefitting their professional growth, they may start to feel like they are mere cogs in a wheel that would be discarded sooner or later. What they do for you today should be a stepping stone in their career progression. Communicate freely, and don't hesitate to show them how you are trying to help them shine.

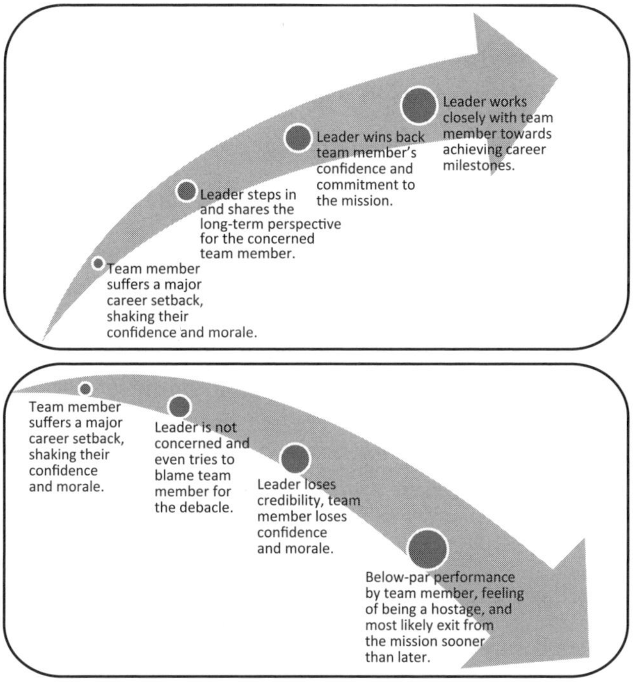

FIGURE 28: **The Cause-Effect Trajectories**

Key Takeaways

- Remember, the happier your team members, the better it is while they are with you and even after they move on.
- To build a connection with your team that goes beyond organisational hierarchy, you need to get inside their hearts and minds.
- As a Credy leader, you need to come up with great what-if scenarios for all your team members and not just those you consider brighter than others.
- All work relationships eventually come to an end, but Credys don't think about this eventuality. They focus on the present and show genuine interest in people's growth and development while respecting their individual circumstances.

Self-Evaluation

Reflect on your contributions to the long-term career growth of your subordinates. Evaluate yourself with the following questions:

- Do you help your team members succeed on the professional front?
- Do you consciously plan and support their career advancement?
- Do you have the courage and sensitivity to stand up for a deserving team member who was denied an opportunity?
- Can you create a motivating roadmap to help a team member bounce back from a stumble in their professional journey?

Now, give yourself Credy Points based on your behaviour in the above context. Pick the appropriate option:

- ○ Always behave like a Credy: 10 Credy points
- ○ Mostly behave like a Credy: 7 Credy points
- ○ Sometimes behave like a Credy, sometimes like a Goofy: 4 Credy points
- ○ Always behave like a Goofy: 0 Credy points

Enabler

'Babu Moshai, Zindagi badi honi chahiye, lambi nahi.'

'Goofy Moshai, Target challenging hona chahiye, unachievable nahi.'

29/36

Smart Leaders, Smart Targets

LET'S ASSUME A fitness coach asks a six-year-old to run 10 kilometres at a stretch and a healthy adult athlete to walk just 100 metres. What will be the impact on the child and the adult? Neither would feel inspired or content. For the child, it would be an impossible goal to achieve, while for the adult it just wouldn't be thrilling enough. Be it sports, business, or life, the goals we set for people greatly influence critical-to-mission factors like buy-in for the target, readiness to meet the target, and passion to carry out the plan. Everyone aspires to be a hero, but the underlying truth is that, to be motivated to give their best, people need targets they can fulfil. This is why leaders need to balance their dream targets with realistic goals. If they don't, those dreams will remain unrealised daydreams.

Businesses have targets and it makes everyone happy when those targets are met. Yet, worldwide, organisations tend to set targets that are designed to fail – they are either too high to be achievable or so low that they make people complacent.

Target-setting is an art and a science, one that is mastered by Credys but completely missed out by Goofys. For one, Credys know how important it is for people to feel successful. They know that if their team members see themselves as winners, they will willingly aim for higher targets. Winners love to break their own record and will do what it takes to continue the winning streak. Credys facilitate this positive loop by setting realistic targets.

Goofys, however, have this incredulous notion that making people feel like failures will drive them to perform. So they purposely set unrealistic targets that create fear, insecurity, and unnecessary pressure. And even when the team manages a win, their Goofy leader will deprive them of any appreciation, because of yet another false belief that praise leads to complacency. Goofys want people to feel like underperformers and underachievers so that they will work harder and make their leader shine in the process.

Unfortunately, these leaders ignore a basic truth – happy employees give better output. And to feel happy and charged-up, people need to feel a sense of contribution and connection to the mission. These emotions cut across age, gender, role, and designation.

Let me share four guiding principles that I apply to target-setting. Feel free to tweak them to your needs.

1. First, targets should be achievable, but not too easily. Set targets that are high enough to push people to their highest potential.
2. Second, each target should have a definite timeline. Take into account all foreseeable opportunities and obstacles but set a deadline.
3. Third, avoid padding up targets based on the assumption that people will not meet the original target anyway. Have faith in your team.
4. Fourth, rather than just dictating numbers, educate people by sharing the logic and data that were used to set the target.

By adopting this four-pronged approach, you will see a greater buy-in from your team. They will enthusiastically make an action plan and then follow it meticulously. You will also see targets being met more often, even if people have to stretch themselves a little.

All in all, regardless of the results, which are governed by many unforeseen factors, sensible target-setting guarantees an exciting and educative experience for your team.

When setting targets, leaders need to remember a fundamental fact: people want to win, but they don't want to win too easily.

Some Goofys take a 'courier service' approach to target-setting. They simply pass down the targets set by their superiors, saying '*Upar se aaya hai*' ('It has come from the top'). How I wish that when their team fails to meet an unrealistic target, they too could ask Goofy to tell senior management: '*Neeche se aaya hai*' ('The performance has come from the bottom').

Goofys also inflate targets arbitrarily. For example, if the goal is to sell a thousand units – which itself would be a first for the organisation – they will, out of habit, add 20 per cent and make it 1,200 units. Conversely, if a target is too low, they will not reset it to a respectable level, because these type of Goofys don't apply their brains at all.

In either case, it's the team that suffers. They either miss the target by a big margin, leaving them demotivated, or achieve it with minimal effort, which gives them no sense of accomplishment. Neither outcome benefits the business.

Setting the right target is half the job done, but only Credys understand this. They see target-setting as an important responsibility that can make or break their reputation as visionary leaders. If needed, they are not afraid to break convention and set their own targets and agendas while staying aligned with the broader vision of the organisation.

This likely explains the unmistakable difference in the happiness and self-esteem quotients of teams led by Credys versus those led by Goofys.

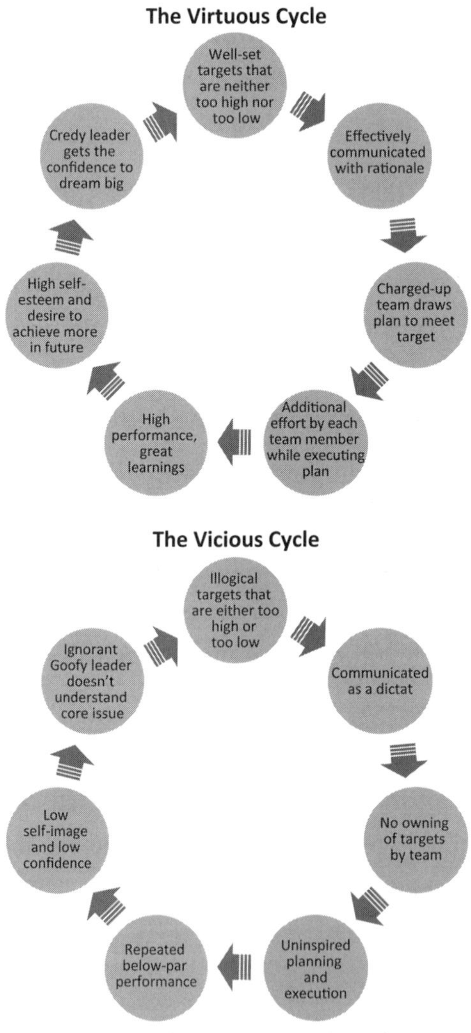

FIGURE 29: **The Virtuous and Vicious Cycles of Target-Setting**

Key Takeaways

- Your team members should be able to feel a sense of achievement, and this is possible only when they are given realistic targets.
- Once you're convinced that a target is attainable and will adequately test your team's competence, sell it to them in a way that inspires them to come on board.
- As the spokesperson for your team, you should have the courage to challenge unrealistic targets.
- Remember, too low a target will create an army of slackers, while too high a target will leave you with a battalion of losers.

Self-Evaluation

Reflect on how smartly you set targets and how well you communicate them to your team. Evaluate yourself with the following questions:

- Do you understand the importance of setting the right targets?
- Do you try to strike a balance between ambitious targets and practical ones?
- Do you realise that while your team members want to win, they don't want to win too easily?
- Do you take the time to explain the reasoning behind the targets set by you?

Now, give yourself Credy Points based on your behaviour in the above context. Pick the appropriate option:

- ○ Always behave like a Credy: 10 Credy points
- ○ Mostly behave like a Credy: 7 Credy points
- ○ Sometimes behave like a Credy, sometimes like a Goofy: 4 Credy points
- ○ Always behave like a Goofy: 0 Credy points

'Tumhara naam kya hai Basanti?'

30/36

Spotting and Taming Confusion Creators

EVERY DISCUSSION, MEETING, or visit has a set agenda. Credible leaders keep people focused on that agenda and guide them to the desired outcome. While the world is already full of distractions, the worst and most avoidable ones come from within the group itself. We all know at least one person who, intentionally or not, asks questions or makes comments that are of little or no importance to the discussion at hand. Some do it to look intelligent; others just enjoy the disruption it creates. If the leader of the group doesn't know how to handle this behaviour, the group can lose focus and the agenda can get derailed.

In every organisation, there are people who thrive on confusion. They can be your team members, colleagues from other departments, or even your seniors. Such people typically create confusion either by asking irrelevant questions or by giving ambiguous answers to others' questions. And they love to watch the effects of their confusing tactics from the sidelines.

Why do some people peddle confusion? What do they get out of it? In my experience, some do it because they genuinely lack the ability to understand things, while others do it simply because they don't want to understand anything. In either case, logic and reasoning don't work with these elements. The risk of engaging with them ranges from losing a precious few hours of your day to ruining your entire workday, and sometimes even more.

Most confusion-mongers don't restrict their tactics to meetings. They do it everywhere – in one-on-one conversations, informal chats, and every other opportunity they get. It's in their DNA!

I once had a colleague who had a habit of approaching our leader with irrelevant 'suggestions' every now and then. For example, when the priority was as micro as the month's sales targets, he would suggest that we study a macro trend like the country's GDP and its impact on consumer behaviour.

On another occasion, during a meeting to improve the capabilities of our sales team, he wanted to discuss the government's new education policy. Basically, he loved asking questions and supplementary questions that were simply no-brainers. His behaviour was not just distracting; it was infuriating.

Our leader, a thorough Credy, came up with a unique solution to this problem. Whenever he found this fellow disrupting a meeting, a presentation, or even the team's general atmosphere with a needless argument, he would join in and add his own views to the argument up to a point. Once he had our colleague's attention, he would start cross-questioning him on the very points raised by him. In the end, he would give the fellow some homework on the topic and ask him to report back within the next few days.

Once, in the middle of an intense discussion on our regional sales strategy, this guy asked if anyone knew the country's GDP for that year vis-à-vis the previous years. Suddenly, people started looking up GDP data on their phones, even when they knew it had no relevance to our very local sales strategy. Noticing the loss of focus, our leader got to work. He asked the confusion-monger to analyse GDP trends of the previous three years, find a correlation between GDP and our sales data for those years, and share his findings within a week.

Our leader summed up this entire exercise as a simple strategy: if you cannot convince a confusion-lover, confuse them back. This saves everyone's time, while the disruptive element gets busy with a task that is non-essential and non-interfering.

This approach eventually transformed our 'topic and time-slayer' colleague into a collaborator, but beware that not everyone will transform so easily. In some cases, you may have to play the 'confuse them back' card for much longer.

An alternative approach: some Credys use silence as a weapon to thwart any attempts to hijack an important discussion. A minute's silence from the leader forces everyone to stop talking, and that's when the leader steers the conversation back to the agenda.

To stop confusion-mongers from destroying your team's focus and productivity, the key is to catch them early and take them to task. But what do you do when your own leader is a confusion-loving character? One of my former leaders belonged to this category of time-wasters, and to the team's poor luck, he found an equal match in one of our colleagues.

Thanks to this pair, our team meetings frequently turned into pointless discussions, where a confusion-loving jerk (our colleague) would raise a useless question and an even bigger jerk (our Goofy leader) would happily take the bait.

Let me share an incident you will find hard to believe, but it actually happened. We were in a team huddle discussing the final preparations for a product launch the next day. A serious discussion was in progress around the guest list, media briefing, speaker notes, logistics, and so on. Suddenly, our colleague rose from his chair and said, 'Before we continue, I've been wondering, if our company wanted to enter a new business, what do you all think it could be?'

It was an utterly irrelevant, confusing, and distracting question, but as always, our leader took the bait. We debated the nonsensical topic for almost an hour, with the discussion being led by none other than our truly Goofy leader.

By the time we were done, there was little time left to discuss the launch. We rushed through the details, which led to many avoidable mistakes during the event. The venue had layout problems, the media briefing was unimpressive, and our leader fumbled during his speech, to name a few.

Mistakes happen, but this was downright reckless. Our Goofy leader had botched up an important event, all because he couldn't resist a pointless distraction. Sadly, such disasters are common in *Goofiland.*

You may ask why the rest of us didn't try to steer the discussion back to the agenda. Well, a bunch of twenty-five-year-olds couldn't say much to a leader who was senior to us in both age and experience.

A lack of focus and not knowing the art of deflection are hallmarks of Goofy leaders. To show off their expertise, they will latch on to any non-issue thrown at them, but it only sows confusion and wastes precious time and resources. It may be a convenient refuge from discussing real challenges and pressing issues, but in the end, it destroys their credibility as leaders who mean business.

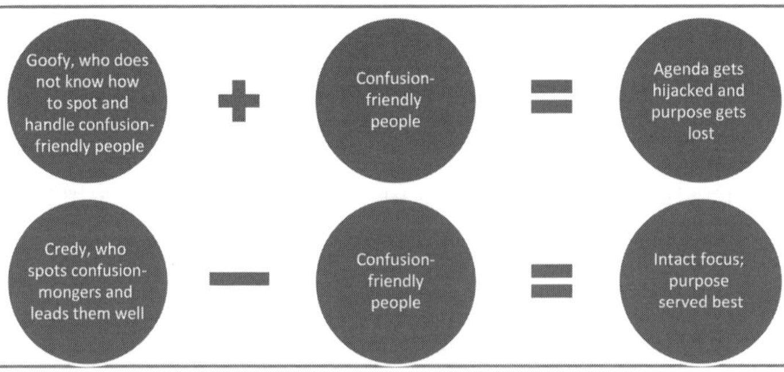

FIGURE 30: **The Confusion Equation**

Key Takeaways

- When leading a discussion, remember the golden rule: not every question needs to be answered and not every point raised is worthy of your time and attention.
- Learn to see through the jerks who try to sidetrack agendas. Don't take the bait!
- Once identified, confusion-friendly colleagues need not be straightened with harsh words. Instead, be quick in dealing with them: hear them out and then immediately put them to task. This might create a little confusion of its own, but it will affect only one person rather than the entire team.

Self-Evaluation

Reflect on your ability to deflect those who deliberately try to sabotage important discussions. Evaluate yourself with the following questions:

- Can you spot a confusion-monger when you come across one?
- Do you manage to thwart attacks on your team's focus and rhythm?
- During meetings, discussions, and presentations, are you able to counter irrelevant arguments that might confuse the group?
- Do you manage to turn the tables on habitual confusion-mongers?

Now, give yourself Credy Points based on your behaviour in the above context. Pick the appropriate option:

- ○ Always behave like a Credy: 10 Credy points
- ○ Mostly behave like a Credy: 7 Credy points
- ○ Sometimes behave like a Credy, sometimes like a Goofy: 4 Credy points
- ○ Always behave like a Goofy: 0 Credy points

*'Pehle apni game baaki logon se unchi karo,
fir apni aawaz unchi karna.'*

31/36

Chaos or Clarity? The Role of Preparedness in Shaping Meetings

IN MANY WAYS, work meetings are no different from a sports match or a live performance. Imagine a player going into a match with absolutely no preparation versus a well-prepared, equally capable opponent; the result is a no-brainer. Similarly, imagine a theatre artist going on stage without preparing the act or rehearsing the dialogues; chances are it will end in disaster not only for the artist but for the co-artists as well. Just as no wise artist or sportsperson will enter the arena unprepared, no good leader enters a meeting without preparation and homework.

Impromptu huddles aside, most meetings are planned in advance and have a clear agenda. But the outcome of any meeting depends on how seriously the participants prepare for it. Anyone who genuinely wants to contribute to the discussion should do the necessary groundwork beforehand.

Credys make it a point to do their homework before important meetings. When they receive an invite to a meeting, they want to know its purpose, the desired outcome, and their expected role in the discussion. Accordingly, they do their prep work. In other words, they don't just attend meetings – they actively participate in the conversation, drive it to relevant points, and ensure that all issues are discussed in the allotted time. Even if every agenda item is not closed, the next steps are usually decided.

Goofys, as you might expect, don't care to do any groundwork even when they have ample advance notice. They walk into meetings unprepared and, depending on the make-up of the group, leave either with an inflated ego or a bruised one. If the group has even one or two sensible people who call out Goofy's causal approach, his ego is done to pieces. But if the group is made up entirely of idiots who support his careless attitude, he gets the validation he is looking for. Either way, the meeting is a disaster.

I learned the power of preparation by observing one of my Credy leaders. Before every important meeting, he made it a point to understand its context, background, and purpose. If something wasn't clear, he did not hesitate to ask the meeting's organiser. After going through the pre-reads and relevant data, he prepared detailed notes, sought inputs from the team, and did further research if needed. Finally, he would write down his opinion along with any questions he wanted to ask during the discussion. When he was the one presenting, he preferred to draft the presentation himself and then asked us to suggest improvements.

With this level of preparation, his presentations were always fluid and impactful and his speech confident and convincing. At times, he had a better grasp of other departments' data and perspectives than their own heads of department. The ripple effect was that his proposals received a favourable nod most of the time.

This preparation-first approach established him as a valuable contributor to strategic meetings.

In any organisation, meetings are happening all the time. Critical decisions are made in these meetings about the organisation's future, cost and revenue projections, course of action, resource allocation (including the most important resource: people), and more. So it is a leader's basic responsibility to make the most of these discussions.

Yet, it's a mystery why Goofys have a casual attitude to meetings. I have seen Goofys walk into meetings without a clue of the who, what, or why of the discussion. They sit there like a piece of furniture or a fly on the wall, looking bored and uninterested and breaking into irrelevant monologues when it's their turn to speak.

Worse, some Goofys open their presentations for the first time in the meeting itself. They try to show it off as being spontaneous, but most people in the room can see through their ill-preparedness. To avoid getting exposed, they rush through the presentation, but this only creates more problems for their team.

When leaders go into meetings unprepared, they fumble and their words lack depth. 'I will get back to you on this' is a common statement from these folks. I have seen even the best orators not know what to say when they are unprepared. Their words simply don't make sense. What they don't realise is that oratory skills can never replace thorough groundwork.

Over time, such Goofys lose credibility as meaningful contributors and are seen as below-average leaders who avoid deep work. Their repeated sloppiness makes them a laughing stock in the organisation. People mock them behind their backs and even wait for them to fumble, stumble, and tumble.

Here, too, it is the team that pays the ultimate price. Whatever they bring to the table bears the stamp of their Goofy leader, as if saying loud and clear, 'Beware, this has come from a team whose leader avoids preparation, does no due diligence, wastes time, and evades real work.' The outcome – their proposals are scrutinised more critically and many are rejected despite being good.

FIGURE 31: **The Credy Preparation-Reward Cycle**

Key Takeaways

- Meetings, conferences, and other professional gatherings are great platforms to build your credibility as a leader. Go into them with a level of readiness that surprises everyone.
- When you are invited to a meeting, not contributing to the discussion can be perceived as disrespect towards the organiser. That said, being respectful should not be your sole reason to prepare for a meeting. Preparation makes meetings productive. Besides, your inputs cement your team's reputation both within the organisation and beyond.
- There may be times when you truly have nothing valuable to add to the discussion, but if this becomes a pattern, you need to ask yourself why.

- Your conduct in meetings and conferences can lay down the carpet for your team or pull it from under their feet. So act accordingly.
- All in all, my advice is to never attend an important meeting unprepared. If you are not ready, either decline the invitation or request a postponement.

Self-Evaluation

Reflect on how well you prepare for strategic meetings and how seriously others take your inputs. Evaluate yourself with the following questions:

- Do you believe it is important for a leader to go into meetings thoroughly prepared?
- Do you value your time enough not to waste it in unproductive discussions?
- Do you understand that your image as a well-prepared leader greatly helps your team?

Now, give yourself Credy Points based on your behaviour in the above context. Pick the appropriate option:

- ○ Always behave like a Credy: 10 Credy points
- ○ Mostly behave like a Credy: 7 Credy points
- ○ Sometimes behave like a Credy, sometimes like a Goofy: 4 Credy points
- ○ Always behave like a Goofy: 0 Credy points

*'Tareekh pe tareekh, tareekh pe tareekh,
tareekh po tareekh milti gayi My Lord,
par insaaf nahi mila.'*

*'Meeting pe meeting, meeting pe meeting,
meeting pe meeting hoti gayi My Lord,
par way forward nahi mila.'*

32/36

Futile Meetings, Empty Results, and the Illusion of Work

Have you ever walked into a meeting with no idea of its agenda or background since neither was ever conveyed to you? Conversely, have you ever walked out of a meeting clueless because the discussion was sloppy and inconclusive? Have you attended a meeting where a lot was discussed and decided, yet nothing was ever implemented? Do you know someone who thinks that organising and attending meetings is the most important part of their job? And have you pretended to be attentive in a meeting when in fact you were clueless about what was being said? I'm guessing you have experienced all of this in abundance. Meetings like this are, without exception, a complete waste of time. I call them 'futureless' meetings – because they don't have any future at all. Your ability to steer clear of such meetings directly speaks to your credibility as a leader who knows his priorities.

One of the biggest time-killers in any organisation is the culture of 'futureless' meetings. Ironically, on one hand, people complain about not having enough time, and on the other, they regularly attend meetings that serve no real purpose.

Futureless meetings are designed to fail. To begin with, many of the participants have no idea why they were invited. The discussion is a drag and, in some cases, even the minutes are not circulated. Worst of all, the points discussed are never followed up and die a natural death over time.

Meetings need time, but we forget that time equals money. Sometimes, a huge amount of money is spent on organising and conducting a meeting. The entire spectacle takes multiple people, dozens of hours, expenses on food, travel, and accommodation, and more. But if the meeting is planned without proper thinking, without selecting the right participants, and without any commitment to the cause, it is a lost investment. The ROI (return on investment) of such meetings runs from zero to negative, especially when you factor in the opportunity cost of so many executives attending a futureless discussion.

While Credys know how to avoid such meetings, Goofys love to both organise and attend them. I, too, have attended my fair share of futureless meetings, until I reached a turning point: I stopped going to meetings unless the purpose, agenda, and expected outcomes were communicated to me in advance.

Credys mean business. For them, meetings are a means to an end, not the end itself.

Goofys mean 'busyness'. For them, meetings are the end itself and just another way to goof around.

Of course, you cannot opt out of every futureless meeting, especially if it is called by a senior leader or a peer. What you *can* do is try and set an example when you are the organiser.

In my experience, people across the hierarchy feel good when decisions made in meetings are put to action. Swiftly sending out minutes of the meeting, with responsibilities and timelines clearly mentioned against each task, keeps people involved and motivated. Additionally, no subsequent meeting on the same topic should begin without a status update. These small actions bring continuity, discipline, and accountability.

An important lesson I learned from one of my leaders was how the composition of a meeting influences its outcome. He strongly believed in inclusivity, but he also believed in keeping the group as small as possible. He avoided inviting people just to make them feel included.

He was also always crystal clear about the agenda and ensured his team did the necessary prework. Pre-reads were shared ahead of time. This made his meetings sharper, shorter, and conclusive.

And he was just as meticulous with post-meeting follow-ups, making sure every agenda item reached a conclusion. People looked forward to attending his meetings, contributing to them, and implementing the decisions taken.

In contrast, a Goofy leader of mine had a strange modus operandi when it came to meetings. He would invite almost everyone to every meeting he organised, including junior employees who had nothing to do with the discussion but could not decline his invitation. With no closures and no follow-ups, these meetings were a complete waste of time. Agenda after agenda was made, meeting after meeting was held, but nothing was ever accomplished.

Eventually, people found a way to avoid this Goofy's meetings. They stopped taking him seriously, stopped coming on time, stopped staying till the end, and you could forget about them contributing to the discussion. Some even started missing critical discussions – ones that drive agendas and initiatives – if they were organised by this Goofy. The reason for this disenchantment was Goofy's lost credibility as a leader who cared about others' time and energy. Sadly, he remained oblivious to the damage.

Based on these varying experiences, I came up with seven Credy principles for organising meetings that need minimum investment and give maximum returns:

1. Set a clear agenda.
2. Invite only relevant participants.
3. Be thorough with your prep work and pre-reads.
4. Start every follow-up meeting with a status update.
5. Ensure timeliness – start, stop, and conclude on time.
6. Circulate minutes of meeting as early as possible.
7. Follow up until all open items are closed.

Quite foolishly, Goofy leaders equate meetings with results. For them, the mere act of organising a meeting is an achievement in itself. You may even find Goofys 'hi-fiving' each other after a meeting just because the meeting happened.

Credys don't have this 'more the merrier' approach to meetings. They are minimalists who treat meetings as a means to an end, and they expect the same from others. This motivates everyone to do their part before, during, and after the meeting.

In the end, these contrasting approaches show up in the results. While Credys achieve success after success, Goofys achieve nothing.

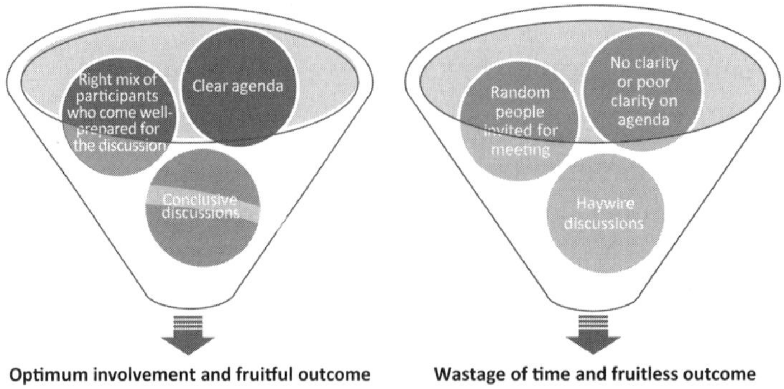

FIGURE 32: **The Meeting Foundry**

Key Takeaways

- For many leaders, work equals meetings, but this mindset is fast losing its appeal.
- Long gone are days when a schedule chock-a-block with meetings was seen as a sign of good leadership. Today's leaders cannot afford to spend all their time in meetings.
- With virtual meetings becoming the norm, it's easier than ever to get caught up in call after call. Learn to choose your battles, because time saved is time gained.
- When invited to a meeting, ask why your presence is required. Let people get used to the idea that you mean business.
- Do not hesitate to be critical of futureless meetings, which you will find in abundance in most organisations.

Self-Evaluation

Reflect on your ability to avoid futureless meetings. Evaluate yourself with the following questions:

- Do you clearly communicate the purpose and agenda of your meetings?
- Do you carefully select the right participants for your meetings?
- Before accepting an invite to a meeting, do you ask for the background and status reports of previous meetings on the subject?
- Do you guide your team on how to identify and avoid futureless meetings?

Now, give yourself Credy Points based on your behaviour in the above context. Pick the appropriate option:

- ○ Always behave like a Credy: 10 Credy points
- ○ Mostly behave like a Credy: 7 Credy points
- ○ Sometimes behave like a Credy, sometimes like a Goofy: 4 Credy points
- ○ Always behave like a Goofy: 0 Credy points

'Kitne aadmi the?'

33/36

The Greats Do Great Follow-Up

YOU MAY THINK leadership is all about giving big speeches or making grand plans, but that's just one part of the job. For a ship's captain, to set sail and then to step aside is to invite disaster. He needs to ensure the ship reaches its destination on time and in the right condition. Similarly, a leader's job doesn't end at setting targets, giving directions, or organising resources. That's just the starting point. His role remains critical until the mission is completed successfully. The leader's continued involvement gives people the energy they need to keep going. And that makes something not-so-glamourous a critical part of the mission: follow-ups.

Millions of organisations and businesses are running in the world and billions of wealth is getting created. This is not just the outcome of a great idea, an impressive mission statement, or a killer business strategy. These elements play their part, but the wheel is turning because someone somewhere is doing the rigour of operationalising these strategies. This part of the process often goes unnoticed when success stories are penned down.

Here's what happens. Once goals are set, strategies laid out, plans made, and roadmaps drawn, a large group of people are given the responsibility to deliver the goals. They have to make the strategy work, execute the plan, follow the roadmap, and achieve the target. These people, who belong to all levels of the hierarchy, work diligently to make the organisation's dream a reality.

In my experience, the big differentiator that decides whether a dream will come true or crash midway is the follow-up done by the group's leader, just like a doctor doing pulse checks on his patients.

Hitting milestones and meeting targets needs rhythmic rigour, and follow-ups are an indispensable part of this rigour. I learned this over many years, when I saw that where follow-ups happened, things moved in the right direction and at the right pace. Otherwise, chaos ruled.

As a leader, regardless of your title, role, or position in the hierarchy, if you want to ensure that the work assigned to your team is actually happening on the ground, you need to track their progress. And this tracking always happens top down.

One of my Credy leaders could be called a master of follow-ups. There are good leaders who know the importance of follow-ups, but they choose to follow up episodically. Then there are great leaders who regularly and consistently track each of their deliverables. And then there are geniuses like my Credy leader, who, with a razor-sharp focus on implementation, track every task, subtask, decision, approval, launch, budget allocation, and everything else with unimaginable vigour and rigour.

At my first follow-up meeting with this leader, I was stunned by his grip on the smallest details. I came out of the meeting in complete awe. When my teammates noticed the look on my face, they just smiled, as if saying, 'Welcome to *Crediverse*!'

This Credy always seemed to know more about the status of our work than we did ourselves. We might miss an action point here or there, but he never did – and he was leading at least a dozen of us. To stay on top of things, he had regular discussions with us and the colleagues supporting us, where he made detailed notes on our ongoing projects.

No matter how small or mundane a task, nothing escaped his attention. He used a simple strategy for this – he ended every meeting by setting a date and time for the next one. This chain of follow-ups was never broken, come what may, and it stopped only when the job was complete.

We had some big product launches, ran countrywide promotions, and chased lofty sales targets under this Credy's leadership. Each of these initiatives involved multiple steps managed by different team members, with our leader carefully overseeing each step. Thanks to his inimitable follow-up skills, we never missed a deadline.

I saw this Credy comfortably manage large teams, multiple projects, and numerous interactions, and I wondered how he did it. I soon realised it was the other way round – he was handpicked for these responsibilities precisely because of his remarkable ability to get things done day in and day out.

Incredibly, he managed all of this without using any sophisticated digital tools. Over the years, I have seen him transition from pen and paper to note-taking apps, which he says has only improved his follow-up capability.

On the other hand, I had a Goofy leader who was 'all *gyan* and no *dhyan*' (lots of talk but zero follow-up). Most of the time, he had no idea what was happening on the projects we were handling. He had all the time to make big speeches but no time for follow-ups. With no grasp over the finer details, he regularly made a fool of himself. And after he had goofed up everything, he would blame us for not doing enough.

I saw a similar display of goofiness in another organisation when a Credy colleague resigned and a Goofy took over his team. Within months, a team that was known to deliver exceptional results started faltering and missing deadlines, all because their new leader had to be fed information like a child.

Let alone handle the smaller issues, this Goofy had no interest even in the big-ticket items. His team's helplessness and frustration were visible to everyone. Slowly, lethargy started to set in, watercooler conversations increased, and a sense of non-contribution became palpable in the team. Some of their brightest performers ended up quitting. But there were also a few smug joes who stayed, revelling in the knowledge that their boss didn't care about their work or even the general state of affairs. They clung to the organisation like well-fed parasites.

In short, what was once *Crediverse* quickly turned into *Goofiland.*

A leader's work is like a river, and each team member's work is a tributary to this river. If the tributaries are not contributing enough water, sooner than later, the river will lose its current. Likewise, if the leader is not good at follow-ups, slippages from the team are not just likely – they are inevitable.

That said, let's not forget that poor follow-up is as good as no follow-up. It leads to last-minute hara-kiri, turning easy situations into high-pressure ones. The team starts to feel like they are on their own with no support from their leader. In the end, nothing gets accomplished, leaving people with a sense of hollowness and unfulfilment.

In any organisation, the ratio of Credys to Goofys in critical leadership roles directly impacts the story that the organisation will write for itself. Even with all the enablers of success in place, if leaders are not doing rigorous follow-ups, things will not move forward.

So roll up your sleeves and make regular follow-ups a habit. You may think I am asking you to micromanage, but I'm not. Following up is just doing your job. It is your duty.

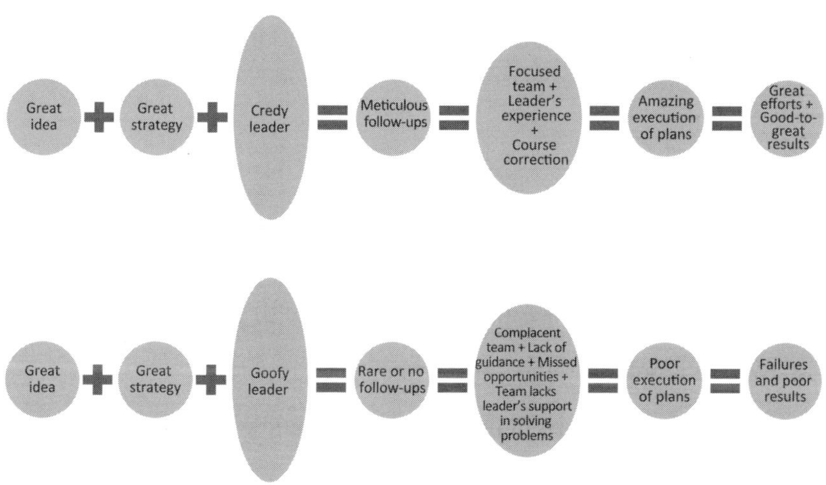

FIGURE 33: **Cause-and-Effect Equation of Follow-ups**

Key Takeaways

- As a credible leader, you cannot afford to be ignorant of the execution status of any project you planned or initiated.
- Don't be a Goofy and hide behind the cliché called delegation. Delegation doesn't mean shirking responsibility.
- To make your follow-ups effective, learn to strike a balance between over-delegation and micromanagement.
- Follow-up is an art, and it needs a great sense of timing – it should be neither too frequent nor too sporadic. You also need to choose the right mode – face-to-face discussions, video calls, or emails – whatever works. Lastly, use the right words – motivate and guide but never belittle. These three aspects – timing, mode, and language – will define whether your follow-ups are seen as helpful guidance or unwelcome interference.

Self-Evaluation

Reflect on how adept you are at timely and meaningful follow-ups. Evaluate yourself with the following questions:

- Do you have regular follow-up meetings with your team?
- Do you regularly review important status reports?
- Do you choose the right frequency, mode, and words for your follow-ups?

Now, give yourself Credy Points based on your behaviour in the above context. Pick the appropriate option:

- ○ Always behave like a Credy: 10 Credy points
- ○ Mostly behave like a Credy: 7 Credy points

- ○ Sometimes behave like a Credy, sometimes like a Goofy: 4 Credy points
- ○ Always behave like a Goofy: 0 Credy points

'Loha garam hai ... Maar do hathoda.'

'Zindagi jeene ke do hi tarike hote hain,
ek jo ho raha hai hone do, bardasht karte jao.
Ya fir zimmedari uthao use badalne ki.'

34/36

Managing Change with Wisdom and Compassion

Imagine you are on a flight and the pilot announces, 'There's a change. We are preparing to make an emergency landing.' That's all – he gives no further details. How would you take this? Your first reaction will be fear, confusion, and helplessness. Now, how would you feel if the pilot adds, 'The emergency landing will be at a nearby airport as no runway is available at the destination. There's nothing to worry, except that your arrival will be delayed by thirty minutes.' You will feel much better, right! The situation is the same, but how it was handled and communicated entirely changed its perception for you.

In corporations, change happens for many reasons: to propel growth, to increase profits, to correct bad decisions, to amplify good business, and so on. Good or bad, small or big, slow or quick – these adjectives can be applied to most changes. Another characteristic of change is that it is inevitable. Whether or not we plan for it, it will happen, and it will affect people in different ways.

One of the key responsibilities of a leader is to manage change effectively. In many cases, it is not the change itself but how it is communicated and executed that determines how people react to it. That is why both communication and execution are critical aspects of change management.

I have had the pleasure of working with Credy leaders who take ownership of change and champion its execution, and they do this with a sense of responsibility towards both their team and the organisation. They take the time to understand the change, and then articulate it clearly without concealing the facts. At the same time, they are mindful of its emotional impact on people.

Conversely, I have also reported to Goofys who only watch the change unfold from a distance. They act as mere messengers of change, rubbing salt on people's wounds with their indifference and casual attitude. They rush to announce the decision just to tick off the task and look efficient to their superiors. Worse, some Goofys sensationalise things by announcing the change like breaking news or, rather, heart-breaking news. They only think about the repercussions of their actions after it's too late, when people have already formed their perceptions and all kinds of corner talks have happened. Changing perceptions at this stage is next to impossible.

Let me be clear. I am in no way suggesting that we should sugar-coat the facts. Rather, it is about being emotionally intelligent and presenting information in the right perspective. It softens the blow and helps people see the long-term value of the change, which may make them more willing to accept it.

Let me tell you about a Credy leader who was excellent at change management. In fact, he had an SOP of his own to handle any big changes in the organisation. First, he would take a deep dive into why the change was happening and how it would take the organisation forward. Then, he would make a list of all his direct and indirect reportees who might be negatively impacted by the change. After carefully analysing the pros and cons for each team member, he would tailor his message for those affected and for the team at large.

In one-on-one conversations, he would address individual concerns while explaining how the organisation was entering a new era that demanded some hard decisions. This helped people see the change in the right light. He would then hold team meetings to formally announce the change. I particularly admired how he handled announcements related to transfers and promotions.

On the other hand, one of my Goofy leaders demonstrated epical levels of goofiness when handling change. A timid character, he never took ownership of unfavourable decisions and instead passed the buck to top management. Worried only for himself, he never bothered to understand the change or communicate it properly to the affected parties. Instead, he would get into needless arguments, even with people who were clear beneficiaries of the change or had nothing to do with it.

At times, he would announce the decision as a broadcast instead of having one-on-one conversations. To this day, I cannot comprehend the level of his goofiness when he announced that our department would be downsized by 80 per cent in the next thirty days. That's it – that's all he said. He had not bothered to get the rest of the information, like why this was being done or what would happen to those being asked to leave. All he gave us was a headline: 'Disaster has struck'. This behaviour is typical of seasoned Goofys.

As a leader, you may not make all the major decisions yourself and, in some cases, you may not even be part of the decision-making process. But that doesn't absolve you of your duty to communicate those decisions to your team in a proper manner. Your credibility is put to test in these defining moments.

Any major change impacts people in both good and bad ways, but a well-thought-out change is generally good for all in the medium to long term. Yet, no matter how hard you try, not everyone will see it that way. There will always be people who feel dissatisfied or sidelined.

This is why you need to ensure that the news lands appropriately with your team. After that, you need to set the right narrative, guide their reactions, and help shape their mindset. In the end, how your team members react to change is critical to their success and, consequentially, to your own success as a leader.

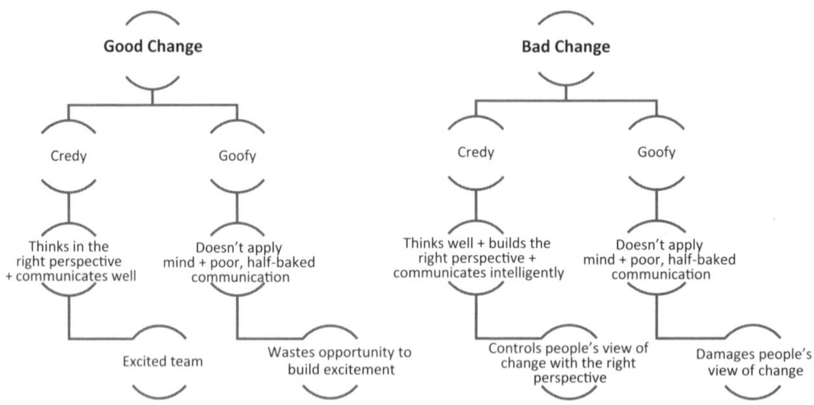

FIGURE 34: **Price and Prize of Change Management**

Key Takeaways

- When confronted with change, face it head-on – you owe it to your team.
- If a change is going to affect your team negatively, you have all the more reason to be present and help them absorb the shock.
- Everyone likes to be the messenger of good news, but only Credy leaders have the courage and sensitivity to announce difficult changes.

- Don't try to flee difficult situations, because all eyes are on you. Nothing will damage your reputation more than an escapist response when you are expected to stay and see things through. A single thoughtless move can position you as a weak, uncaring, and incompetent leader.
- Take ownership of change whether or not you had a role in the decision. Choose your words carefully when explaining the rationale behind it. The right approach will strengthen your team's perception of you as a leader.

Self-Evaluation

Reflect on how effectively you manage change, particularly when it might negatively affect some or all of your team members. Evaluate yourself with the following questions:

- Do you communicate change in the right perspective?
- Do you tend to disown hard decisions even if you were party to them?
- Are you able to foresee the impact of a major change and prepare your team members for the same?

Now, give yourself Credy Points based on your behaviour in the above context. Pick the appropriate option:

- ○ Always behave like a Credy: 10 Credy points
- ○ Mostly behave like a Credy: 7 Credy points
- ○ Sometimes behave like a Credy, sometimes like a Goofy: 4 Credy points
- ○ Always behave like a Goofy: 0 Credy points

'Jail me surang ban chuki hai...'

35/36

Rumour Management: Diligence versus Indulgence

When people work together in large groups, stories and rumours are bound to emerge. These grapevine tales have a life of their own. They make the rounds, become magnified, and eventually die out or become legends. Rumours can be personal, professional, or a mix of both, and they are laced with juicy details. So, yes, they are tempting, but they're also addictive. You might indulge in them for fun, but you will soon be addicted and ultimately branded a rumour-monger. The best way is to stay away.

It would not be an overstatement to say that rumours are in the DNA of every organisation. Nor would it be an exaggeration to say that some people spend the majority of their workday gossiping. They are either spreading rumours or creating new ones. The survival of these rumour-mongers depends on how much dirt they can dig up.

The worst hit in this game are the ones being talked about, but the rumour-mongers are not spared either. They don't realise that anyone who discusses a rumour even offhandedly is seen as a catalyst in spreading it. The damage to their reputation is multi-fold – they are seen as time-wasters, rumour-spreaders, and de-focused, among other things.

This makes rumour management a necessity for leaders who don't want their team members to be seen as irresponsible gossipers.

Credy leaders are acutely aware of the threatening potential of grapevine culture. They are, plain and simple, not interested in unconfirmed stories that don't concern them. But Goofys are wily characters who pounce upon rumours. They will go from desk to desk or make call after call to relay juicy tales. Their closed-door conversations almost always revolve around gossip, and even their team discussions are laced with baseless stories. This is how a few 'bad apples' end up manipulating perceptions by peddling unverified facts. Credy leaders know that it is all counterproductive and not worthy of their time and energy.

Let me share how a Credy and a Goofy dealt with the same rumour that was making the rounds in our organisation. We heard that a leader was being transferred midyear, which was unusual, and there were whispers that the reason was underperformance. The gentleman in question was a peer of both my direct leader, a classic Credy, and another leader, a typical Goofy.

Sensing the uncalled-for curiosity in our team, my leader called a quick meeting. He asked us to immediately stop discussing the matter, and he explained why: 'First of all, feel free to ask me any questions you have about this issue. But you must stop discussing it among yourselves or with others. You will only waste time over something that doesn't concern you at all. Also, you might end up saying something that could later be used against you. And let's not forget, when you show interest in rumours, you give the impression that you are more interested in gossip than your work, which is not good at all for your personal and professional image. No one sees a gossiper in good light.'

This one conversation changed the environment within the team. The speculations simply stopped and everyone went back to work. The only victim in this case was the rumour itself – it died a quiet death and its soul departed from *Crediverse* for good.

This incident apart, our Credy leader never encouraged us to bring rumours to him even when they were related to our work. Whenever some hearsay surfaced, his formula was simple: if needed, let's talk to the right people at the right time and get the right information. This fact-check mechanism helped in two ways: if the rumour concerned our work, learning the truth saved us from worrying about how the rumour might affect us. If the rumour wasn't related to our work, knowing the facts put our curiosity to rest once and for all.

The Goofy leader handled the situation differently. He gladly gossiped about the rumoured transfer with anyone and everyone. Even worse, he gave his team members a petty task: mingle with others to dig up more details. He was so goofed up that he had no idea what a bad example he was setting.

No wonder, this Goofy was fond of those who brought him spicy details of others' miseries. His 'sources' were either weak characters like him or smart joes who took advantage of his obsession with gossip by feeding him what they liked. He made numerous Goofy decisions as a result.

In the long run, such leaders and their loyal subjects end up the same way – stuck in inconsequential roles and assignments.

As a leader, you need to be aware of the grapevine around you. You cannot control rumours from germinating, but you can create a firewall around your team by building a solid anti-rumour culture. It's a subjective call when to ignore such talks and when to deal with them head on. In other words, you need to know the tipping point after which you must act.

Straight talk with the rumour-mongering team member and getting the facts out is how Credys deal with such situations.

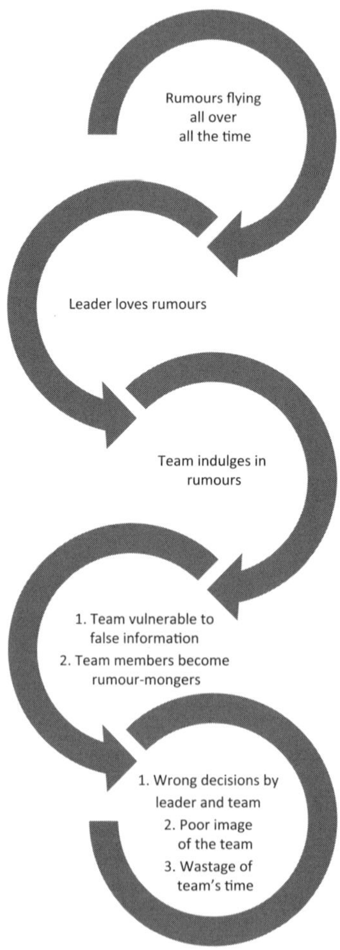

FIGURE 35: **The Downward Spiral of Rumour-mongering**

Key Takeaways

- Rumour management is an opportunity to save your team's time, energy, and focus.
- Cultivate a culture of non-indulgence in rumours. Lead from the front by showing your team that you don't care about gossip.
- Learn to handle rumours the right way. If it doesn't matter, don't waste your time on it. If it matters at all, don't handle it like a conspiracy. In other words, either discuss it threadbare or don't discuss it at all.
- Want to know the facts? Don't waste time in tea-room talks and go straight to the person who knows the truth.

Self-Evaluation

Reflect on your rumour-management abilities as a leader. Evaluate yourself with the following questions:

- Do you see rumours as a waste of time or as a source of entertainment?
- Do you have the self-control to avoid indulging in hearsay?
- Do you make sure your team members refrain from rumour-mongering?
- Do you have the skill to end a rumour that's affecting your team negatively?

Now, give yourself Credy Points based on your behaviour in the above context. Pick the appropriate option:

- ○ Always behave like a Credy: 10 Credy points
- ○ Mostly behave like a Credy: 7 Credy points
- ○ Sometimes behave like a Credy, sometimes like a Goofy: 4 Credy points
- ○ Always behave like a Goofy: 0 Credy points

The power of saying No.

36/36

Personal Space: Why Goofys Can't Respect Boundaries

ALL OF US need personal space where we can do what we like or believe in. Here, by space, I don't just mean physical space but also emotional and mental space. The sign at the entrance to this space is – or should be – loud and clear: 'Do not enter without permission. Trespassers will be prosecuted.' Credible leaders respect this boundary and do not breach it unless allowed to. Goofys, on the contrary, feel entitled to barge into people's personal space whenever they like. They act as if it is their birthright to know everything about their subordinates, including their private lives. They will give you unsolicited 'friendly' advice on every matter just to prove their superiority and wisdom. But these leaders forget that being friendly is not the same as being friends. While being friendly with your colleagues is welcome and even encouraged, being friends is altogether different, and it is rare in the leader-follower relationship.

Before we talk more about respecting personal space, let's be clear that getting to know your team members or their families is not the problem here. To a large extent, it is a very credible thing to do. The problem arises when you fail to respect people's personal time, choices, and beliefs and attack them with your own opinions just to have more control over them.

In my experience, many leaders don't realise that respect for an individual and respect for his personal space are one and the same thing. The moment you breach someone's personal space, you have disrespected the person. Some common examples are calling or texting your team members in their personal time; interfering in their family matters; passing judgement on their friends, food choices, modes of entertainment, social media usage, personal travel, body weight, habits, fitness routine, shopping behaviour, finances, family members, the pets they keep, or anything that does not concern you or the work they do for you.

Remember, no personal comment or opinion is required from you unless explicitly requested, or in exceptional circumstances when a team member's personal commitment might overlap with a project deadline. Even then, a credible leader limits his opinion to what is absolutely necessary. For example, if a team member applies for leave to attend a family celebration, you may ask him to prioritise pending tasks and, if needed, to reconsider the length of the leave. That's it.

When it comes to respecting personal boundaries, I have had all sorts of experiences with leaders I have worked with or observed from a distance. While Credys respected their team members' personal space, Goofys invaded it left, right, and centre.

One of my Credy leaders, who was extremely mindful of others' personal space, taught me many lessons through his *Crediniyat*. When I first joined his team, he made a conscious effort to get to know me, my family, my daily routine, personal preferences, and so on.

He did the same with my colleagues. For example, if he knew someone was taking guitar lessons before coming to work, he would try and avoid early morning meetings that might force the person to miss the class.

He also deeply valued rest and recovery. He never emailed us on weekends. In fact, he would stop sending emails from Friday afternoon itself. Instead, he would write the email and schedule it for Monday morning. With this simple act, he showed us how much he respected our personal space. He knew that receiving an email on the weekend would force people to act even if it wasn't urgent, or it would at least occupy their minds and disrupt their me-time.

There were many other thoughtful gestures. For example, he never offered advice on personal matters unless asked. When we had meals together and everyone ordered what they liked, he never commented on who was eating what, unlike many Goofys I have shared team lunches with. He treated us like grown-ups, not as children who should be told what they should or should not eat. While he was super fit himself, he never passed judgement on anyone's diet, weight, or lifestyle.

Now, before you start to see this as a lack of concern on his part, let me clarify that this behaviour only earned him immense respect from the team. We loved working with this Credy. Many of us went to him with personal issues, because we were sure of two things – that he would be discreet and that he would never cross the line even when we gave him the right to do so.

On the other end of the spectrum, I had a Goofy leader who had an opinion on everything and advice for everyone. He was quite weak at his work and a hardcore Goofy in many other ways, but his *Goofaniyat* crossed all limits when it came to respecting personal boundaries. He thought of himself as some kind of genius on life. Yes, you read that right – a genius on life who believed he knew everything under the sun and the moon.

Apart from asking prying questions about our family members, he loved to tell us which school to choose for our children, what foods to eat, whom to befriend, where to go on vacation, which movies to watch, which brands to buy, where to buy property, which stocks to invest in, which rituals to follow, and what not. He even gave family planning advice to those who cared to listen. Once, he went to the extent of calling a team member's wife to tell her what meals to cook so her husband would be more energetic at work.

As if this wasn't enough, he would force us to like his posts on LinkedIn, even though he rarely had anything good to say about anything. I once travelled with him on a business trip, and the moment we stepped out of the airport, the first thing he criticised was the airport itself. According to him, one of the best airports in the country, appreciated far and wide for its modern architecture and convenient design, had not been planned well.

I had another Goofy leader who had a problem with any of his team members being free and happy. His sole aim in life was to overburden us with work while we were in the office and even afterwards. It was normal for us to receive calls from him at odd hours. If someone was going on a holiday, he would deviously assign them more work. Ridiculously, most of this extra work included tasks that could have easily waited a few days, could have been planned better, or, worst, were not needed at all. Basically, he found sadistic pleasure in leaving us with no time for our personal commitments or interests.

This Goofy had such a negative vibe that his entry into any office party was a mood spoiler for everyone. He could not see people having a good time, so he would pass sarcastic remarks like 'If you had shown the same energy at work, you would have met your targets by now.'

These were just a few ways he encroached upon our personal time and tested our sanity. Some of it may sound unbelievable, but anyone who has worked with a Goofy knows that such leaders can stoop to any level to prove their supremacy.

Eventually, breach after breach of personal boundaries left our Goofy leader with no credibility. Once it was clear that he had no respect for us and no regard for our physical or mental well-being, following him became a mere compulsion. People avoided him, lied to him when they needed a day off, and hated him to the best of their abilities.

Key Takeaways

- Be mindful of physical and emotional boundaries to maintain comfort and respect at work.
- Respect personal time and support flexible schedules to help your team maintain a healthy work-life balance.
- Be approachable, but maintain professional boundaries to ensure fairness and objectivity.
- Respect privacy. Offer advice only when asked, and listen with empathy.

Self-Evaluation

Reflect on your willingness to allow personal space to your team members. Evaluate yourself with the following questions:

- Do you think your team should be available to you 24X7?
- Do you avoid making comments about your team members' personal choices?

- Do you believe in giving advice on personal matters only when asked?
- Do you feel that you know everything about everything?
- Do you feel that being a leader gives you the right to know every personal detail about your team members?

Now, give yourself Credy Points based on your behaviour in the above context. Pick the appropriate option:

- ○ Always behave like a Credy: 10 Credy points
- ○ Mostly behave like a Credy: 7 Credy points
- ○ Sometimes behave like a Credy, sometimes like a Goofy: 4 Credy points
- ○ Always behave like a Goofy: 0 Credy points

Epilogue

IT BREAKS MY heart to see people suffer for two reasons:

- They have a Goofy leader they have to deal with every day.
- Even the most well-intentioned leaders struggle to become Credy leaders, simply because they don't know how to go about it.

I have myself faced both situations in my professional life. Fortunately, I have also seen plenty of Credy leaders in action – the delight they bring to the workplace and the lives they enrich.

It was both the pain and delight from these experiences that motivated me to write this book.

I am deeply passionate about helping people reach their full potential, and I will feel accomplished if this book helps even one person adopt credible behaviour and build a solid reputation as a Credy leader.

The Path to Credibility

As you may have realised while reading this book, my vision of a Credy leader is not just about excelling in a profession, business, or other pursuit. It is about being an *exceptionally credible leader*

– a leader who is secure, trusted, admired, resourceful, dependable, and surrounded by competent followers.

Becoming a true Credy needs mental toughness and self-conditioning. Unlike making a plan or executing a strategy, it is an ongoing process that takes time. As leaders, we are all works in progress, but with enough practice, Credy behaviour can become our second nature.

A Note for Experienced Leaders

As a seasoned leader reading this book, you may have found yourself thinking, 'Wow, that's exactly what I would do in this situation!' At the same time, you may have discovered a few things you are not doing or may be doing incorrectly. These areas can be turned into quick wins that will make you an even more effective leader.

A Note for Emerging Leaders

If you are in the early stages of your career or you are not yet leading a team, this book has given you a head start on building your credibility as a leader. By adopting credible behaviour right from the start, you will set a strong foundation for your leadership journey.

The Bottom Line

Every now and then, a leader is faced with two choices: the easy one and the right one. The key is to choose like a Credy even when the odds are stacked against you.

Pre-launch Feedback from Readers

Let me quickly share feedback from the pre-launch readers of this book. Since you may have had similar thoughts while reading the book, each remark is followed by a response from me.

- '*They [the 36 credibility traits] look easy.*'

  They might look easy, but they are not so easy to practise.

- '*I think I already practise these mantras like a Credy.*'

  Be honest with yourself; there is a good chance you are wrong.

- '*I feel that most of my peers are Goofys.*'

  You may be right!

- '*After reading this book, I realised that most of my leaders have been Goofys.*'

  You may be right.

- '*I've had at least one leader who was a full Credy. Even my current leader is almost a Credy.*'

  Send a thank-you note to each of those leaders, along with a copy of this book.

A Promise of Continued Learning

This book is a compilation of everything I've learned so far about being a credible leader. But the journey doesn't end here. I promise to keep learning and sharing new insights with you.

I would love to hear your thoughts on the book. Do write to me at *rohit@rohitgoel.co.in* or *roship2001@gmail.com*.

I wish you all the best on your journey to becoming an incredible leader by being credible. For sure, you are going to touch hundreds of lives leaving a profound impact on them.

It is my hope and wish that someday someone among your followers will dedicate their own *Credified* leadership style to you.

Be authentic. Be credible!

The Credification Playbook: Turning Ideas into Actions

(100 minutes per quarter)

This playbook is intended to Credify leaders like you in a simple and practical way.

If you have gone through the 36 traits of a credible leader and believe that credibility can be the ultimate multiplier for all your other leadership skills like vision, intelligence, and communication, I highly recommend that you use this playbook for at least one year. It will help you assess yourself, plan the changes you want to make, and systematically adopt credible behaviour through consistent practice.

Here you go! Your 12-month Credification journey in three simple steps.

How to Use This Playbook

Take a deep breath and start with these steps:

Step 1: Measure Your CLB (Credible Leadership Behaviour) Score

- Give yourself Credy Points for each of the 36 Credibility traits discussed in this book. Select the option that best reflects your behaviour:

- ○ Always behave like a Credy: 10 Credy points
- ○ Mostly behave like a Credy: 7 Credy points
- ○ Sometimes behave like a Credy, sometimes like a Goofy: 4 Credy points
- ○ Always behave like a Goofy: 0 Credy points

- Record your scores in the 'Score' column of the Diagnosis and Adoption Tool (Annexure A).
- Once you have done this for all 36 traits, you will get your Credible Leadership Behaviour score. The maximum CLB score is 360 and the minimum is 0.

Step 2: Make Your Adoption Plan

- Reflect on your areas of improvement and note them in the 'Reflect – What is Missing' column.
- Think about the changes you want to make and note them in the 'Adopt – What I Will Do' column.

Step 3: Mark Your CLB Score on the Credimeter

A tool called the Credimeter (Annexure F) will be your companion on this journey. Mark your CLB score on the Credimeter. This will place you in one of the following leadership zones:

CLB Score	Leadership Zone	What It Means
271–360	Credy Zone	You are a highly credible leader.
151–270	Croofy Zone	Your leadership style is a mix of credible and not-so-credible behaviours.
0–150	Goofy Zone	Knowingly or unknowingly, you are operating like a Goofy.

Adoption Period

After completing Step 3, start adopting the behavioural changes you committed to in Step 2.

From day to day, you will encounter various situations at work. Some will be similar to those included in this book, others will be entirely new. Your Adoption Plan, along with your learnings from this book, will be your guide in handling these situations.

Once you start to think and act like a Credy, your decisions will be in the right direction.

Sustaining Momentum

To see results, repeat Steps 1–3 every three months for at least one year. Continue to practise credible behaviour along the way. After one year, I leave it to you to continue using this playbook.

Over the course of the year, your Credification journey will look like this:

Quarter 1 (Annexure A)

- **Step 1:** **M**easure your CLB (Credible Leadership Behaviour) score
- **Step 2:** **M**ake your adoption plan
- **Step 3:** **M**ark your CLB score on the Credimeter
- Start practising the traits and behaviours you have resolved to adopt.

Quarter 2 (Annexure B)

- Repeat Steps 1–3.
- Continue practising Credy behaviour and make improvements where needed based on new insights.

Quarter 3 (Annexure C)

- Repeat Steps 1–3.
- Continue practising Credy behaviour and make improvements where needed based on new insights.

Quarter 4 (Annexure D)

- Repeat Steps 1–3.
- Continue practising Credy behaviour and make improvements where needed based on new insights.

Your Year-Long Credification Journey

	Use Playbook and Complete Steps 1-3			Use Playbook and Complete Steps 1 3			Use Playbook and Complete Steps 1-3			Use Playbook and Complete Steps 1-3			
	Month 1	***Month 2***	***Month 3***	***Month 4***	***Month 5***	***Month 6***	***Month 7***	***Month 8***	***Month 9***	***Month 10***	***Month 11***	***Month 12***	
	Adopt the new behaviour			Adopt the new behaviour			Adopt the new behaviour			Adopt the new behaviour			
Credification Journey starts	**Sprint 1**			**Sprint 2**			**Sprint 3**			**Sprint 4**			***Credified!*** **Keep up the good work, sustain and improve your Credy score.**

Smart Tips

- When rating yourself on the 36 Credibility traits, use the Self-Evaluation questions at the end of each chapter as a guide.
- Refer to the illustration of the Diagnosis and Adoption Tool for guidance (Annexure E).
- For assistance on how to use the Credimeter, refer to the illustration of Credimeter (Annexure G).
- Remember the golden rule for using this tool: do not lie to yourself. Rate and reflect with truth and honesty.

Golden Tip

You can use this playbook to help your team members evaluate themselves and make their own adoption plans.

Fun Tips

- Use this playbook to assess the leaders you have come across in your career and see where their fit.
- Organise a group activity where participants evaluate a common leader to see how different people perceive the same individual.

Now that you've come this far, let's define your unique Leadership Brand and Values.

What's Your (Leadership) Brand Story?

Let's summarise your aspirational brand story.

Your Tagline

____

____

Example 1: 'I will help people meet their targets, overcome challenges, and grow as leaders.'

Example 2: 'I will build a strong team that willingly takes on new challenges while creating value for the organisation.'

Values you want to be known for

1. ______________________________________
2. ______________________________________
3. ______________________________________
4. ______________________________________
5. ______________________________________

Examples:

1. Impartial
2. One who honours commitments
3. An authentic storyteller

Your Leadership Poster

Create a Leadership poster with your tagline and values. Frame or laminate it and put it up where you can see it every day. Remember, just like food and water, inspiration is something you need every day!

(Your Name)

____

____

My Leadership Tagline

____

____

Values I want to be known for

1. ___________________________________
2. ___________________________________
3. ___________________________________
4. ___________________________________
5. ___________________________________

Acknowledgements

First of all, my deepest thanks to my Mother, who laid the foundation for the person I have become.

I'm grateful for the journey of the past few decades, which gave me the opportunity to meet some of the finest leaders in their fields, and some not-so-fine ones too.

My sincere thanks to my friends Udit Jain, Nandita Tiwari, Tanay Tarany, Rahul Agarwal, Richa Gupta, Deepika Aggarwal, Salil Narang, Madhura Kulkarni, and Sachin Samar for reading the beta versions of this book and helping me with your merciless feedback ☺. Gratitude to my English teacher, Ms Janaki Kharkwal Ma'am, for giving me the gift of language.

Special thanks to my dear friends Sarang Kayande, Sunil Verma, Anuj Lakhanpal, Vishal Bhatnagar, Anand Nautiyal, Ravi Danturty, Anjali Sharma, Amit Raju, Karan Markan, Parag Aggarwal, Tanuj Jain, and Gaurav Gupta for always standing by me.

Great thanks to Neetu Ralhan, the editor of this book, for not only her professional editing but also being a trusted advisor on every aspect of book writing and pulishing. Your nudges of feedback brought the book back on track several times during my journey of writing it.

Finally, to my wife, Shipra, and my daughters, Radhikaa and Ridhimaa. Thank you for giving me the space, support, and environment to write this book. Your patience, encouragement, and honest critiques kept me going. Radhikaa, you've set an example by being credible in your role as President of National Service Scheme at college. Ridhimaa, you are the clearest thinker I know, and you've shown me how a class monitor can also be a Credy one.

Annexure A

Diagnosis and Adoption Tool (Sprint 1)

Date: **Name of Leader:**

S.No.	Chapter Title	Trait	Score	Reflect – What Is Missing	Adopt – What I Will Do
1	Leading with High Personal Standards	Reflect on your personal standards around discipline, ethics, and integrity.			
2	Honouring Commitments: A Matter of Life and Death	Reflect on how much you value your own words and whether you realise the importance of fulfilling your commitments as a leader.			
3	The Credy-Goofy Divide: Transparency versus Manipulation	Reflect on how honestly you present subpar performance, whether your own or that of those reporting to you.			
4	Secure Credys versus Insecure Goofys	Reflect on how you handle feelings of insecurity and self-doubt as a leader.			
5	Law of Attraction	Reflect on how rational you are when selecting people or service providers for a job.			
6	Nostalgia Gone Wrong: Goofys Who Live in the Past	Reflect on how remaining stuck in the past may keep you from adapting to new realities.			
7	The Fine Line between Having Favourites and Practising Favouritism	Reflect on how your personal preferences could blur the line between valuing individuals and showing unfair favouritism.			
8	Breaking Protocol the Right Way	Reflect on how you break protocols. Is it to serve a higher purpose or for ulterior motives?			
9	Easy Exits	Reflect on how you react to people leaving your team.			
10	Shared Triumphs	Reflect on how you share success – do you celebrate triumphs together or keep credit for yourself?			
11	From Praise to Power: Turning Foes into Allies	Reflect on how much you use genuine praise to transform adversaries into allies.			

12	Backfired Decision? Just Disown It! A Classic Goofy Escape	Reflect on how you respond to failed decisions – do you take ownership or disown responsibility?			
13	From Confusion to Clarity: How Credys Cut Through Jargon	Reflect on how much you simplify complexity for others and create clarity around you.			
14	Workplace Surveys: Fair or Farcical?	Reflect on how open and receptive you actually are to honest feedback from your team.			
15	Failing Boldly: Cultivating Fearlessness from Setbacks	Reflect on how you treat failures of your team members – as sources of fear or as bold learning opportunities.			
16	The Goofy Trap of Unrealistic Commitments	Reflect on how realistic you are in making commitments and setting expectations.			
17	Image Matters!	Reflect on how your image is positioned within the organisation.			
18	Hostility-Free Zone: Creating a Safe Space for Your Team	Reflect on how consciously you create a safe, hostility-free environment for your team.			
19	Turning Trouble into Triumph: The Power of Credys	Reflect on how you turn troubles into opportunities for team growth and resilience.			
20	Tough Conversations to Address Unprofessional Behaviour and Underperformance	Reflect on how you handle tough conversations to address challenging behaviours of your team members.			
21	The Art of Recharging Morale After a Setback	Reflect on how you rekindle team morale and hope after setbacks.			
22	Anti-Monotony: How Credys Sustain Motivation in Repetitive Work	Reflect on how you keep your team's motivation high, even in repetitive tasks.			
23	Learning and Development: How Goofys Prevent Progress	Reflect on how proactively you develop your team members.			
24	Anticipating Opportunities: How Credys Stay Ahead of the Pack	Reflect on how you anticipate and prepare for emerging opportunities before others.			
25	Mastering Feedback	Reflect on how effectively you give feedback.			

26	Fake Praise vs Authentic Appreciation	Reflect on how authentic and impactful your appreciation is, versus giving shallow praise.			
27	Logic, Research, and Experience: Three Pillars of a Solid Action Plan	Reflect on how you put effort in building logic, research, and experience in decision-making.			
28	Igniting Aspirations for Long-Term Success	Reflect on how you ignite and support team members' long-term aspirations and ambitions.			
29	Smart Leaders, Smart Targets	Reflect on whether you set smart targets for your team.			
30	Spotting and Taming Confusion Creators	Reflect on how you spot and handle confusion creators in your workspace.			
31	Chaos or Clarity? The Role of Preparedness in Shaping Meetings	Reflect on how your preparedness shapes the clarity and effectiveness of meetings.			
32	Futile Meetings, Empty Results, and the Illusion of Work	Reflect on how you ensure meetings produce meaningful results, not just the illusion of work.			
33	The Greats Do Great Follow-Up	Reflect on how consistently you follow up to deliver on promises.			
34	Managing Change with Wisdom and Compassion	Reflect on your approach to managing and communicating change.			
35	Rumour Management: Diligence versus Indulgence	Reflect on how diligently you manage and address rumours rather than indulge them.			
36	Personal Space: Why Goofys Can't Respect Boundaries	Reflect on whether you respect personal and professional boundaries at work.			
Credible Leadership Behaviour (CLB) Score					

Annexure B

Diagnosis and Adoption Tool (Sprint 2)

Date: **Name of Leader:**

S.No.	Chapter Title	Trait	Score	Reflect – What Is Missing	Adopt – What I Will Do
1	Leading with High Personal Standards	Reflect on your personal standards around discipline, ethics, and integrity.			
2	Honouring Commitments: A Matter of Life and Death	Reflect on how much you value your own words and whether you realise the importance of fulfilling your commitments as a leader.			
3	The Credy-Goofy Divide: Transparency versus Manipulation	Reflect on how honestly you present subpar performance, whether your own or that of those reporting to you.			
4	Secure Credys versus Insecure Goofys	Reflect on how you handle feelings of insecurity and self-doubt as a leader.			
5	Law of Attraction	Reflect on how rational you are when selecting people or service providers for a job.			
6	Nostalgia Gone Wrong: Goofys Who Live in the Past	Reflect on how remaining stuck in the past may keep you from adapting to new realities.			
7	The Fine Line between Having Favourites and Practising Favouritism	Reflect on how your personal preferences could blur the line between valuing individuals and showing unfair favouritism.			
8	Breaking Protocol the Right Way	Reflect on how you break protocols. Is it to serve a higher purpose or for ulterior motives?			
9	Easy Exits	Reflect on how you react to people leaving your team.			
10	Shared Triumphs	Reflect on how you share success – do you celebrate triumphs together or keep credit for yourself?			
11	From Praise to Power: Turning Foes into Allies	Reflect on how much you use genuine praise to transform adversaries into allies.			

12	Backfired Decision? Just Disown It! A Classic Goofy Escape	Reflect on how you respond to failed decisions – do you take ownership or disown responsibility?			
13	From Confusion to Clarity: How Credys Cut Through Jargon	Reflect on how much you simplify complexity for others and create clarity around you.			
14	Workplace Surveys: Fair or Farcical?	Reflect on how open and receptive you actually are to honest feedback from your team.			
15	Failing Boldly: Cultivating Fearlessness from Setbacks	Reflect on how you treat failures of your team members – as sources of fear or as bold learning opportunities.			
16	The Goofy Trap of Unrealistic Commitments	Reflect on how realistic you are in making commitments and setting expectations.			
17	Image Matters!	Reflect on how your image is positioned within the organisation.			
18	Hostility-Free Zone: Creating a Safe Space for Your Team	Reflect on how consciously you create a safe, hostility-free environment for your team.			
19	Turning Trouble into Triumph: The Power of Credys	Reflect on how you turn troubles into opportunities for team growth and resilience.			
20	Tough Conversations to Address Unprofessional Behaviour and Underperformance	Reflect on how you handle tough conversations to address challenging behaviours of your team members.			
21	The Art of Recharging Morale After a Setback	Reflect on how you rekindle team morale and hope after setbacks.			
22	Anti-Monotony: How Credys Sustain Motivation in Repetitive Work	Reflect on how you keep your team's motivation high, even in repetitive tasks.			
23	Learning and Development: How Goofys Prevent Progress	Reflect on how proactively you develop your team members.			
24	Anticipating Opportunities: How Credys Stay Ahead of the Pack	Reflect on how you anticipate and prepare for emerging opportunities before others.			
25	Mastering Feedback	Reflect on how effectively you give feedback.			

26	Fake Praise vs Authentic Appreciation	Reflect on how authentic and impactful your appreciation is, versus giving shallow praise.			
27	Logic, Research, and Experience: Three Pillars of a Solid Action Plan	Reflect on how you put effort in building logic, research, and experience in decision-making.			
28	Igniting Aspirations for Long-Term Success	Reflect on how you ignite and support team members' long-term aspirations and ambitions.			
29	Smart Leaders, Smart Targets	Reflect on whether you set smart targets for your team.			
30	Spotting and Taming Confusion Creators	Reflect on how you spot and handle confusion creators in your workspace.			
31	Chaos or Clarity? The Role of Preparedness in Shaping Meetings	Reflect on how your preparedness shapes the clarity and effectiveness of meetings.			
32	Futile Meetings, Empty Results, and the Illusion of Work	Reflect on how you ensure meetings produce meaningful results, not just the illusion of work.			
33	The Greats Do Great Follow-Up	Reflect on how consistently you follow up to deliver on promises.			
34	Managing Change with Wisdom and Compassion	Reflect on your approach to managing and communicating change.			
35	Rumour Management: Diligence versus Indulgence	Reflect on how diligently you manage and address rumours rather than indulge them.			
36	Personal Space: Why Goofys Can't Respect Boundaries	Reflect on whether you respect personal and professional boundaries at work.			
Credible Leadership Behaviour (CLB) Score					

Annexure C

Diagnosis and Adoption Tool (Sprint 3)

Date: **Name of Leader:**

S.No.	Chapter Title	Trait	Score	Reflect – What Is Missing	Adopt – What I Will Do
1	Leading with High Personal Standards	Reflect on your personal standards around discipline, ethics, and integrity.			
2	Honouring Commitments: A Matter of Life and Death	Reflect on how much you value your own words and whether you realise the importance of fulfilling your commitments as a leader.			
3	The Credy-Goofy Divide: Transparency versus Manipulation	Reflect on how honestly you present subpar performance, whether your own or that of those reporting to you.			
4	Secure Credys versus Insecure Goofys	Reflect on how you handle feelings of insecurity and self-doubt as a leader.			
5	Law of Attraction	Reflect on how rational you are when selecting people or service providers for a job.			
6	Nostalgia Gone Wrong: Goofys Who Live in the Past	Reflect on how remaining stuck in the past may keep you from adapting to new realities.			
7	The Fine Line between Having Favourites and Practising Favouritism	Reflect on how your personal preferences could blur the line between valuing individuals and showing unfair favouritism.			
8	Breaking Protocol the Right Way	Reflect on how you break protocols. Is it to serve a higher purpose or for ulterior motives?			
9	Easy Exits	Reflect on how you react to people leaving your team.			
10	Shared Triumphs	Reflect on how you share success – do you celebrate triumphs together or keep credit for yourself?			
11	From Praise to Power: Turning Foes into Allies	Reflect on how much you use genuine praise to transform adversaries into allies.			

12	Backfired Decision? Just Disown It! A Classic Goofy Escape	Reflect on how you respond to failed decisions – do you take ownership or disown responsibility?			
13	From Confusion to Clarity: How Credys Cut Through Jargon	Reflect on how much you simplify complexity for others and create clarity around you.			
14	Workplace Surveys: Fair or Farcical?	Reflect on how open and receptive you actually are to honest feedback from your team.			
15	Failing Boldly: Cultivating Fearlessness from Setbacks	Reflect on how you treat failures of your team members – as sources of fear or as bold learning opportunities.			
16	The Goofy Trap of Unrealistic Commitments	Reflect on how realistic you are in making commitments and setting expectations.			
17	Image Matters!	Reflect on how your image is positioned within the organisation.			
18	Hostility-Free Zone: Creating a Safe Space for Your Team	Reflect on how consciously you create a safe, hostility-free environment for your team.			
19	Turning Trouble into Triumph: The Power of Credys	Reflect on how you turn troubles into opportunities for team growth and resilience.			
20	Tough Conversations to Address Unprofessional Behaviour and Underperformance	Reflect on how you handle tough conversations to address challenging behaviours of your team members.			
21	The Art of Recharging Morale After a Setback	Reflect on how you rekindle team morale and hope after setbacks.			
22	Anti-Monotony: How Credys Sustain Motivation in Repetitive Work	Reflect on how you keep your team's motivation high, even in repetitive tasks.			
23	Learning and Development: How Goofys Prevent Progress	Reflect on how proactively you develop your team members.			
24	Anticipating Opportunities: How Credys Stay Ahead of the Pack	Reflect on how you anticipate and prepare for emerging opportunities before others.			
25	Mastering Feedback	Reflect on how effectively you give feedback.			

26	Fake Praise vs Authentic Appreciation	Reflect how authentic and impactful your appreciation is, versus giving shallow praise.			
27	Logic, Research, and Experience: Three Pillars of a Solid Action Plan	Reflect on how you put effort in building logic, research, and experience in decision-making.			
28	Igniting Aspirations for Long-Term Success	Reflect on how you ignite and support team members' long-term aspirations and ambitions.			
29	Smart Leaders, Smart Targets	Reflect on whether you set smart targets for your team.			
30	Spotting and Taming Confusion Creators	Reflect on how you spot and handle confusion creators in your workspace.			
31	Chaos or Clarity? The Role of Preparedness in Shaping Meetings	Reflect on how your preparedness shapes the clarity and effectiveness of meetings.			
32	Futile Meetings, Empty Results, and the Illusion of Work	Reflect on how you ensure meetings produce meaningful results, not just the illusion of work.			
33	The Greats Do Great Follow-Up	Reflect on how consistently you follow up to deliver on promises.			
34	Managing Change with Wisdom and Compassion	Reflect on your approach to managing and communicating change.			
35	Rumour Management: Diligence versus Indulgence	Reflect on how diligently you manage and address rumours rather than indulge them.			
36	Personal Space: Why Goofys Can't Respect Boundaries	Reflect on whether you respect personal and professional boundaries at work.			
	Credible Leadership Behaviour (CLB) Score				

Annexure D

Diagnosis and Adoption Tool (Sprint 4)

Date: **Name of Leader:**

S.No.	Chapter Title	Trait	Score	Reflect – What Is Missing	Adopt – What I Will Do
1	Leading with High Personal Standards	Reflect on your personal standards around discipline, ethics, and integrity.			
2	Honouring Commitments: A Matter of Life and Death	Reflect on how much you value your own words and whether you realise the importance of fulfilling your commitments as a leader.			
3	The Credy-Goofy Divide: Transparency versus Manipulation	Reflect on how honestly you present subpar performance, whether your own or that of those reporting to you.			
4	Secure Credys versus Insecure Goofys	Reflect on how you handle feelings of insecurity and self-doubt as a leader.			
5	Law of Attraction	Reflect on how rational you are when selecting people or service providers for a job.			
6	Nostalgia Gone Wrong: Goofys Who Live in the Past	Reflect on how remaining stuck in the past may keep you from adapting to new realities.			
7	The Fine Line between Having Favourites and Practising Favouritism	Reflect on how your personal preferences could blur the line between valuing individuals and showing unfair favouritism.			
8	Breaking Protocol the Right Way	Reflect on how you break protocols. Is it to serve a higher purpose or for ulterior motives?			
9	Easy Exits	Reflect on how you react to people leaving your team.			
10	Shared Triumphs	Reflect on how you share success – do you celebrate triumphs together or keep credit for yourself?			
11	From Praise to Power: Turning Foes into Allies	Reflect on how much you use genuine praise to transform adversaries into allies.			

12	Backfired Decision? Just Disown It! A Classic Goofy Escape	Reflect on how you respond to failed decisions – do you take ownership or disown responsibility?			
13	From Confusion to Clarity: How Credys Cut Through Jargon	Reflect on how much you simplify complexity for others and create clarity around you.			
14	Workplace Surveys: Fair or Farcical?	Reflect on how open and receptive you actually are to honest feedback from your team.			
15	Failing Boldly: Cultivating Fearlessness from Setbacks	Reflect on how you treat failures of your team members – as sources of fear or as bold learning opportunities.			
16	The Goofy Trap of Unrealistic Commitments	Reflect on how realistic you are in making commitments and setting expectations.			
17	Image Matters!	Reflect on how your image is positioned within the organisation.			
18	Hostility-Free Zone: Creating a Safe Space for Your Team	Reflect on how consciously you create a safe, hostility-free environment for your team.			
19	Turning Trouble into Triumph: The Power of Credys	Reflect on how you turn troubles into opportunities for team growth and resilience.			
20	Tough Conversations to Address Unprofessional Behaviour and Underperformance	Reflect on how you handle tough conversations to address challenging behaviours of your team members.			
21	The Art of Recharging Morale After a Setback	Reflect on how you rekindle team morale and hope after setbacks.			
22	Anti-Monotony: How Credys Sustain Motivation in Repetitive Work	Reflect on how you keep your team's motivation high, even in repetitive tasks.			
23	Learning and Development: How Goofys Prevent Progress	Reflect on how proactively you develop your team members.			
24	Anticipating Opportunities: How Credys Stay Ahead of the Pack	Reflect on how you anticipate and prepare for emerging opportunities before others.			
25	Mastering Feedback	Reflect on how effectively you give feedback.			

26	Fake Praise vs Authentic Appreciation	Reflect on how authentic and impactful your appreciation is, versus giving shallow praise.			
27	Logic, Research, and Experience: Three Pillars of a Solid Action Plan	Reflect on how you put effort in building logic, research, and experience in decision-making.			
28	Igniting Aspirations for Long-Term Success	Reflect on how you ignite and support team members' long-term aspirations and ambitions.			
29	Smart Leaders, Smart Targets	Reflect on whether you set smart targets for your team.			
30	Spotting and Taming Confusion Creators	Reflect on how you spot and handle confusion creators in your workspace.			
31	Chaos or Clarity? The Role of Preparedness in Shaping Meetings	Reflect on how your preparedness shapes the clarity and effectiveness of meetings.			
32	Futile Meetings, Empty Results, and the Illusion of Work	Reflect on how you ensure meetings produce meaningful results, not just the illusion of work.			
33	The Greats Do Great Follow-Up	Reflect on how consistently you follow up to deliver on promises.			
34	Managing Change with Wisdom and Compassion	Reflect on your approach to managing and communicating change.			
35	Rumour Management: Diligence versus Indulgence	Reflect on how diligently you manage and address rumours rather than indulge them.			
36	Personal Space: Why Goofys Can't Respect Boundaries	Reflect on whether you respect personal and professional boundaries at work.			
Credible Leadership Behaviour (CLB) Score					

Annexure E

Illustration of Diagnosis and Adoption Tool

Date: **Name of Leader:**

S.No.	Chapter Title	Trait	Score	Reflect – What Is Missing	Adopt – What I Will Do
1	Leading with High Personal Standards	Reflect on your personal standards around discipline, ethics, and integrity.	7	Not much is missing but, yes, I am habitually non-punctual.	I am committed to enhancing my time management skills and I resolve never to take people for granted, valuing their time as much as my own.
2	Honouring Commitments: A Matter of Life and Death	Reflect on how much you value your own words and whether you realise the importance of fulfilling your commitments as a leader.	7	Sometimes I overestimate my resources and hence overcommit.	Before committing, I will make extra effort to ascertain that I have adequate resources to fulfil the commitment.
3	The Credy-Goofy Divide: Transparency versus Manipulation	Reflect on how honestly you present subpar performance, whether your own or that of those reporting to you.	0	I hide poor performance by not showing the data in an ideal way. Also, I do blame other departments unjustifiably for my failures.	I will be very open and reflective about my own achievements or failures.

Annexure F
Credification Journey Tracker
Credimeter

Name of Leader:

Mark Yourself

360	Credy Zone				
350					
340					
330					
320					
310					
300					
290					
280					
270	Croofy Zone				
260					
250					
240					
230					
220					
210					
200					
190					
180					
170					
160					
150	Goofy Zone				
140					
130					
120					
110					
100					
90					
80					
70					
60					
50					
40					
30					
20					
10					
0					
	Date				
	CLB Score				
	Sprint No.	1	2	3	4

Annexure G

Credification Journey Tracker

Illustration of Credimeter

Name of Leader:

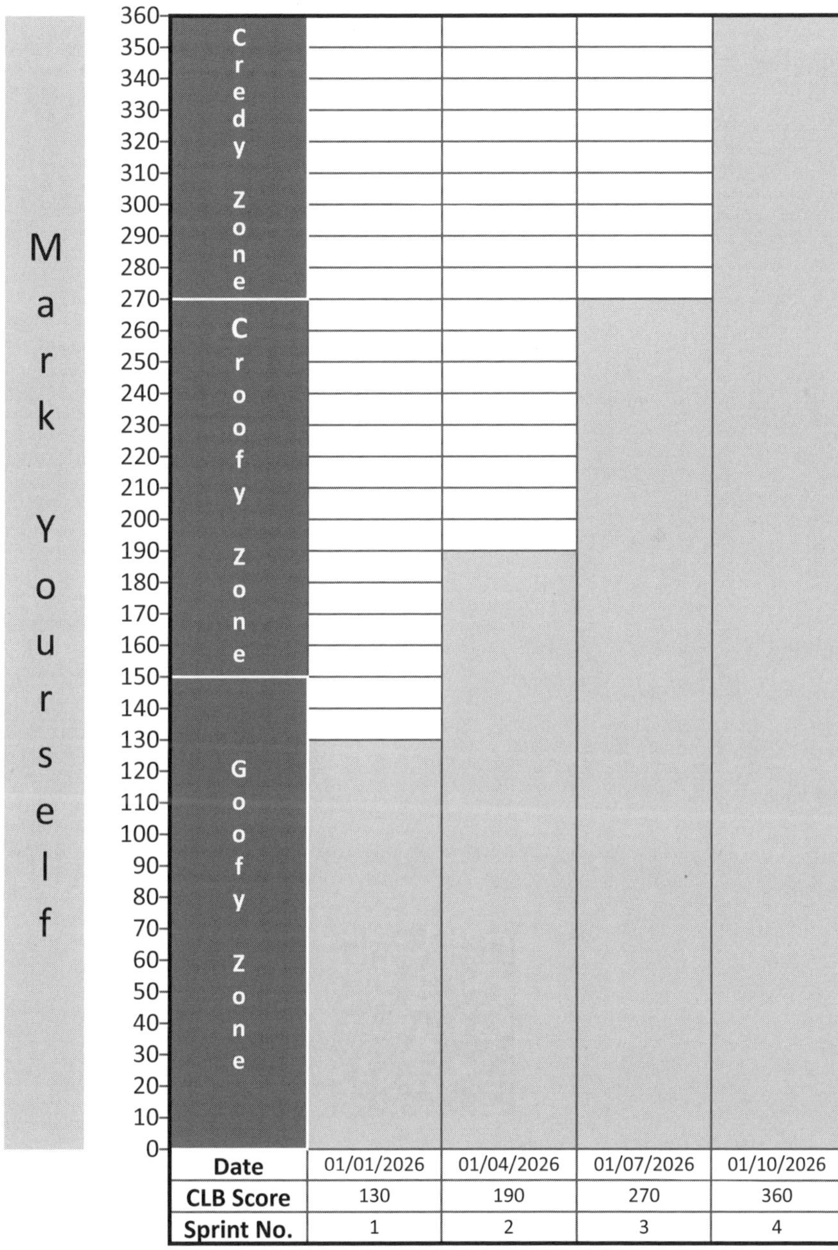

Date	01/01/2026	01/04/2026	01/07/2026	01/10/2026
CLB Score	130	190	270	360
Sprint No.	1	2	3	4

Scan the QR code to download the
Playbook Tools

Other Books by Rohit Goel

- 📖 **A Story of Resilience & Reinvention**
  A powerful, true-to-life narrative about bouncing back after a corporate layoff — when falling is inevitable, but failing is not.

- 💼 **Inspired by Real Experiences**
  Written by an industry veteran who witnessed the shutdown of a global automobile company in India and the emotional aftershocks that followed.

- 🧠 **What Really Happens Behind the Pink Slip**
  Through the diary of Vikram, a fired Vice President, the book explores 36 days of emotional turmoil, betrayal, clarity, and eventual growth.

- 🛠 **Skills & Connections – Your Career Safety Net**
  Offers sharp insights on how to safeguard yourself against career setbacks by building the right capabilities and networks.

- 🧘 🎭 **Beyond Corporate – A Human Story**
  Speaks directly to the mental, emotional, and social impact of job loss — something rarely acknowledged in corporate narratives.

- 🧭 **For Everyone in the Game of Careers**
  Whether you're a professional, spouse, entrepreneur, student, or a leader — this book will resonate with you deeply.

- 🏆 **An Amazon #1 Bestseller**
  Widely appreciated by readers across all walks of life — from freshers to founders — and available in Kindle and paperback on Amazon.in.

"माँ" सिर्फ एक किताब नहीं, एक एहसास है — एक श्रद्धांजलि उस ममता, शक्ति और प्यार को, जो हमें गहराई से छूते हैं।

इस काव्य-संग्रह में मैंने और मेरी बेटी ने मिलकर दो पीढ़ियों की भावनाओं को शब्दों में ढालने की कोशिश की है — सरल, सच्ची और सहज भाषा में।

- **सादा लेकिन असरदार भाषा**

  इन कविताओं की भाषा वही है जो हम रोज़मर्रा में बोलते हैं — एक खूबसूरत मिश्रण है हिंदी, अंग्रेज़ी, उर्दू और फ़ारसी के शब्दों का, जो बात को दिल से कहने में मदद करते हैं।

- **😄 भावनाओं का रंगमंच — कभी मुस्कुराहट, कभी प्रेरणा**

  इसमें आपको मिलेंगी कुछ कविताएँ जो दिल से हँसाती हैं, कुछ जो प्रेरित करती हैं, और कुछ जो चुपचाप आपको सोचने पर मजबूर कर देती हैं।

- **👨‍👧 पिता-बेटी की साझा आवाज़**

  यह संग्रह एक अनोखा संवाद है — दो पीढ़ियाँ, नज़रिए, पर भावनाएँ एक जैसी। ज़िंदगी के कई रंग इन पन्नों पर मिलते हैं — माँ-बच्चे का रिश्ता, दोस्ती, प्रेम, संघर्ष और आत्मबोध।

- **🌸 सांस्कृतिक स्पर्श**

  भारतीय संस्कृति, सिनेमा, त्योहार, खाना, और हमारा सामाजिक व्यवहार — ये सब इस संग्रह में झलकते हैं, जो इसे साहित्यिक ही नहीं, दिल से जुड़ा हुआ अनुभव बनाते हैं।

- **📖 हर कविता — एक अनुभूति, एक कहानी**

  चाहे वो नौकरी की उलझन हो या माँ की गोद की शांति, हर कविता किसी न किसी जानी-पहचानी भावना से जुड़ी है। ये शब्द बस पढ़े नहीं जाते, महसूस किए जाते हैं।

"माँ" आपको न सिर्फ़ एक साहित्यिक अनुभव देती है, बल्कि अपने रिश्तों और जीवन को नई नजर से देखने की प्रेरणा भी देती है।

Credits for Film Dialogues and Images (Presented as Illustrations) Used in this Book

1. *'Main aaj bhi pheke hue paise nahin uthata'*: **Deewar** (1975) produced by Gulshan Rai.
2. *'Parampara. Pratishtha. Anushasan. Yeh is gurukul ke teen stambh hai'*: **Mohabbatein** (2000) produced by Yash Chopra.
3. *'Ek baar jo maine commitment kar diya, fir main apne aap ki bhi nahin sunta'*: **Wanted** (2009) produced by Boney Kapoor.
4. *'Johny bure kaam toh karta hai lekin imaan ke saath'*: **Johny Mera Naam** (1970) produced by Gulshan Rai.
5. *'Mujhe joh sahi lagta hai main karta hoon ... wo chahe bhagwan ke khilaaf ho, samaaj ke khilaaf ho, police, kanoon ... ya phir poore system ke khilaaf kyun na ho'*: **Sarkar** (2005) produced by Ram Gopal Varma.
6. *'Don ka intezaar toh baarah mulko ki police kar rahi hai, but Don ko pakadna mushkil hi nahi, namumkin hai!'*: **Don** (1978) produced by Nariman Irani.
7. *Your vibe attracts your tribe*: **Lagaan** (2001) produced by Aamir Khan.
8. *'Crime Master Gogo naam hai mera, aankhen nikal ke gotiyan khelta hun main'*: **Andaz Apna Apna** (1994) produced by Vinay Sinha.
9. *'Wo jaisa bhi hai mera putr hai'*: **Mahabharat** (1988) produced by B.R. Chopra.
10. *'Logon ko haque jamana aata hai rishta nibhana nahi'*: **Karwaan** (2018) produced by Ronnie Screwvala and Priti Gupta.
11. *'Jaa Simran jaa, ji le apni zindagi!'*: **Dilwale Dulhania Le Jayenge** (1995) produced by Yash Chopra.
12. *'Kamaal is baat ka nahin hai Shekhar ki usne wo zameen khali karva di ... kamaal ye hai ki wo janta tha ki wo ye sab kuch kar sakta tha ... Ye aadmi zindagi mein kuch na kuch karega'*: **Trishul** (1978) produced by Gulshan Rai.
13. *'Insaan ka kartavya hota hai koshish karna ... kaamyabi nakaamyabi sab Uske haath mein hai'*: **Zindagi Na Milegi Dobara** (2011) produced by Farhan Akhtar and Ritesh Sidhwani.
14. *'Arre bhai kehna kya chahte ho ...'*: **3 Idiots** (2009) produced by Vidhu Vinod Chopra.
15. *'Bada aadmi agar banna ho, toh choti harkatein mat karna'*: **Vidhata** (1982) produced by Gulshan Rai.
16. *'Bade bade deshon mein aisi chhoti-chhoti baatein hoti rehti hain,* Senorita': **Dilwale Dulhania Le Jayenge** (1995) produced by Yash Chopra.
17. *'Ek chutki sindoor ki keemat tum kya jaano Ramesh Babu'*: **Om Shanti Om** (2007) produced by Gauri Khan.
18. *'Sara sheher mujhe Lion ke naam se janta hai'*: **Kalicharan** (1976) produced by N.N. Sippy.

19. *'Ye dhai kilo ka haath jab kisi pe padta hai na, to aadmi uthta nahin, uth jaata hai'*: **Damini** (1993) produced by Ravi Chopra.
20. *'Jali ko aag kehte hain, bujhi ko raakh kehte hain, jis raakh se barood bane usey Vishwanath kehte hain'*: **Kalicharan** (1976) produced by N.N. Sippy.
21. *'Woh do the aur tum teen, phir bhi wapas aa gaye khaali haath. Kya samajh kar aaye the? Sardar bahot khus hoga? Sabasi dega?'*: **Sholay** (1975) produced by G.P. Sippy.
22. *'How's the josh!'*: **Uri: The Surgical Strike** (2019) produced by Ronnie Screwvala.
23. *'Sattar minute, sattar minute hain tumhare paas ...'*: **Chak De! India** (2007) produced by Aditya Chopra.
24. *'Har bachche ki apni khoobi hoti hai, apni kaabliyat hoti hai, apni chahat hoti hai'*: **Taare Zameen Par** (2007) produced by Aamir Khan.
25. *'Bhagwan ke bharose mat baithiye, kaa pata bhagwan humre bharose baitha ho'*: **Manjhi – The Mountain Man** (2015) produced by Manish Mundra and team.
26. *'Bachcha kabil bano, kabil ... kamyabi to sali jhak maar ke peeche bhagegi'*: **3 Idiots** (2009) produced by Vidhu Vinod Chopra.
27. *'Moonche hon to Nathulal jaise hon ... warna na hon'*: **Sharaabi** (1984) produced by Prakash Mehra.
28. *'Mogambo khush hua!'*: **Mr. India** (1987) produced by Boney Kapoor.
29. *'Taqat to gainda bhi lagata hai, lekin sher lagata hai taqat aur technique dono ... sher ban'na hai, gainda nahin'*: **Dangal** (2016) produced by Aamir Khan, Kiran Rao and Siddharth Roy Kapur.
30. *'Picture abhi baaki hai mere dost!'*: **Om Shanti Om** (2007) produced by Gauri Khan.
31. *'Babu Moshai, Zindagi badi honi chahiye, lambi nahi'*: **Anand** (1971) produced by Hrishikesh Mukherjee.
32. *'Tumhara naam kya hai Basanti?'*: **Sholay** (1975) produced by G.P. Sippy.
33. *'Pehle apni game baaki logon se unchi karo, fir apni aawaz unchi karna'*: **Chak De! India** (2007) produced by Aditya Chopra.
34. *'Tareekh pe tareekh, tareekh pe tareekh, tareekh pe tareekh milti gayi My Lord, par insaaf nahin mila!'*: **Damini** (1993) produced by Ravi Chopra.
35. *'Kitne aadmi the?'*: **Sholay** (1975) produced by G.P. Sippy.
36. *'Loha garam hai ... Maar do hathoda'*: **Sholay** (1975) produced by G.P. Sippy.
37. *'Zindagi jeene ke do hi tarike hote hain – ek jo ho raha hai hone do, bardasht karte jao. Ya fir zimmedari uthao use badalne ki'*: **Rang De Basanti** (2006) produced by Rakeysh Omprakash Mehra.
38. *'Jail me surang ban chuki hai ...'*: **Sholay** (1975) produced by G.P. Sippy.
39. *The power of saying No*: Image from **Pink** (2016) produced by Rashmi Sharma.